Poems from the Heart

A Collection of Poems for Midlife Women...

...to ease the menopausal journey...

You Are Not Alone...

Dr. Renata Shiloah

Nutritionist4u, Inc.

Disclaimer

The poetry contained in this book is provided for entertainment and feel-good purposes only. Please consult your physician for treatment options for any condition.

Used by permission. All rights reserved.
ISBN: 979-8-218-30097-5
Cover design by Micky Shiloah
Proofreading by vocem LLC
www.nutritionist4u.com

ATTENTION: SCHOOLS AND BUSINESSES
Dr. Renata Shiloah's books are available at quantity discounts for educational, business, or sales promotional use. For more information, send an email to
drrenatashiloah@nutritionist4u.com

*"To all remarkable midlife women.
I hope you find solace, inspiration, strength, and beauty
within you through the pages of this book."*

With love and gratitude,

Dr. Renata Shiloah

Praise for *Poems From the Heart*

'Poems from the Heart' beautifully intertwines personal experiences and eloquent poetry, serving as a reassuring companion for those navigating midlife's challenges. These verses resonate with the author's intimate midlife journey, offering solace and solidarity to readers at this pivotal stage. With its gentle, rhythmic words, the book guides you toward renewed confidence, joy, and serenity, reminding you that you're not alone. Each page reveals a kindred spirit who understands midlife complexities, providing refuge, inspiration, and renewal for women in this phase of life. 'Poems from the Heart' is not only a testament to the enduring power of words and the human spirit, inviting you to rediscover your inner strength, but it is also a heartfelt companion on your midlife journey, offering hope and a profound connection, and is a timeless addition to the world of midlife exploration.

Dr. Amie DCN, CFMP *'The Thyroid Fixer'*

This book is a gift to all women. The poems are beautifully written and deeply insightful, and they capture the full range of emotions women experience during menopause, from joy to sorrow to frustration. This book is a must-read for any woman who wants to understand and celebrate this critical life transition.

Kristi C. *Austin TX, 'Fellow Menopause Warrior'*

'Poems from the Heart' is a beautiful tribute to womanhood and the time of life known as menopause. This book is uplifting and encourages women to look at themselves and this season of life as not a curse but a journey. I found myself smiling as I read the heartfelt words on each page. Dr. Shiloah motivates the reader to grab onto each moment of life and see beauty. This book is a must-read for women of all ages.

Leigh Ricard, *Jacksonville, Fl, "Fellow Menopause Warrior'*

Dr. Renata writes from her heart in a book that spans decades. This thoughtful compilation of poetry written from the perspective of a young adult and then spanning through the many stages of life addresses love, loneliness, and rebirth during midlife. Dr. Shiloah shares her innermost thoughts, utilizing the magic of poetry to reach a broad audience of women facing similar struggles to provide a shared sense of community and hope. I recommend this touching and empowering book for women going through changes during midlife land to their partners, families, and friends who may also gain a better understanding of what their mothers, sisters, and friends may be experiencing.

Betty Nadby, *LCSW-R*

Dr. Renata is one of her field's most celebrated, intelligent, and esteemed professionals. She remains open and expansive, perpetually learning and discovering new ways to share her expertise with midlife women, including colleagues, patients, family, and friends. She effortlessly blends clinical and professional knowledge with personal experiences, allowing readers to feel seen, heard, encouraged, and inspired. Through her empowering poems, inspiring affirmations, and powerful reflections, Dr. Shiloah guides readers through the challenging experience of menopause. Through her literary work, she further proves her ability to gently yet confidently call out topics typically not otherwise discussed, creating and holding space for midlife women to validate their related yet individual experiences while also receiving support and encouragement.

Allison Thomas, *LCSW, Psychotherapist, Usui Shiki Ryoho Reiki Practitioner*

A STORY FROM MY HEART TO YOURS

My story began at age twelve when those unpredictable hormones started wreaking havoc on my life. PMS was no picnic, but little did I know that perimenopause would come roaring in like a storm. I hoped everything would return to normal once I hit menopause, but reality hit me hard. Those hormones seemed to be lifelong companions, and I battled severe symptoms for most of my adult life. This tumultuous journey inspired me to write the self-help book **"It's Time For A PAUSE."** The prospect of entering midlife filled me with dread. Then, one day, my children stumbled upon a hidden treasure - a journal containing a poetry book I had written at age twelve when my hormonal rollercoaster began. Publishing those heartfelt poems had always been a dream of mine, and now that dream has finally materialized.

"Poems from the Heart" is a collection of emotional verses from my soul, capturing the sadness, highs, and lows I experienced even at that young age. Life can be challenging, especially in midlife. However, I've learned that there's always something we can discover to make each phase worthwhile. For me, becoming a grandmother was a profound blessing during midlife. Using the joy of that experience to guide me toward better emotional well-being and maintaining a healthy diet, exercise routine, and sufficient sleep has been the key to my overall health. I sincerely hope you find solace in this book and discover the one thing that can keep you sane during this stage of life because you deserve to live your best life ever!

Dr. Renata Shiloah

Table of Contents

Table of Contents (Continued)

Table of Contents (Continued)

Table of Contents (Continued)

Table of Contents (Continued)

Table of Contents (Continued)

Poems From the Heart

Introduction

This book is a companion to my empowering self-help boo
'It's Time For a PAUSE.' Women are warriors, yet there's n
need to endure the challenges of our midlife journeys alone.
Let's elevate the importance of menopause awareness
together. Inside this book, you'll discover a treasure trove o
'202' poems, each written from my heart to yours.

My choice of *'202'* poems is no coincidence; in numerology
this angelic number signifies rebirth from and a welcoming
embrace of a new, transformative journey. Ladies, embrace
your inner warrior, and let's embark on this enlightening
voyage together!

Facebook -Support Group
TikTok
Instagram
Amazon
'It's Time For A PAUSE' -self-help book
 Lucy Blue Eyes Series

Use the QR code below to access free resources and suppo
www.nutritionist4u.com

It's Time For a PAUSE!

It's Time for a PAUSE!
Let's win this battle together,
Take a Breath--And Remember
You are Never Alone--
My Fellow Menopause Warrior!

Everything BAD is for Something GOOD

Everything bad is for something good.
Everything has a purpose
that can be understood.

Everything bad can lead to
happiness and bliss.
It's all up to us—
to what we dismiss.

Count your blessings,
for they are always with you.
Everything has a reason.
Everything doesn't have to be blue.

*In honor of my beloved mother, Jarmila
Shayo, who always saw the light within the
darkness. I offer this poem as a dedication to
her enduring spirit and wise words.*

Self-Reflection

Midlife
a threshold of self-reflection,
where dreams and realities
find connection.
In the mirror,
lines of experience show,
a journey traveled,
with much left to grow.
Embracing changes,
a newfound stride,
midlife's wisdom,
a beacon to guide.

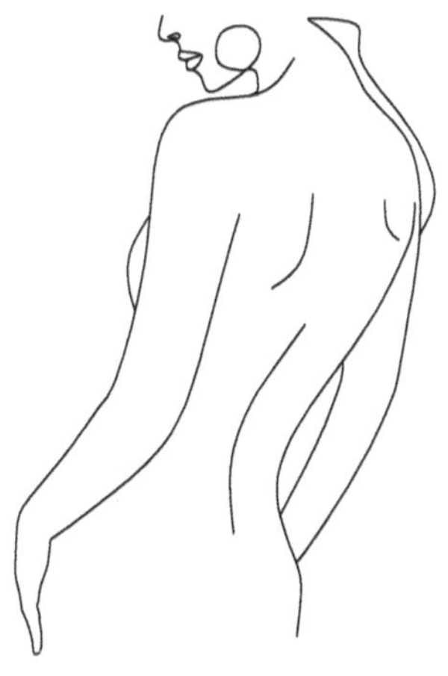

Freedom's Reign

Menopause,
the gateway to freedom's reign,
a metamorphosis where we break the chain.
No longer bound by monthly ebb and flow,
we embrace the freedom that our spirits know.

No more whispers of youthful expectations,
we step into ourselves
as authentic creations.
A symphony of liberation,
loud and clear . . .
Menopause, the anthem of freedom,
we cheer.

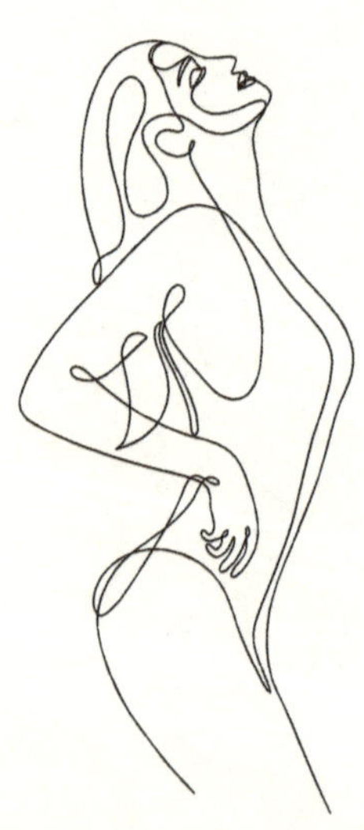

The Arrival

Menopause arrives,
a joyful shift in our stride
embracing the changes,
with hearts open wide.
No longer bound,
we embrace newfound bliss,
radiating strength,
in this chapter we'll miss.
We celebrate freedom,
with hearts all aglow,
happy in our essence,
as women, we grow.

Amid Change

Amid change,
we find our bliss.
Menopause,
a journey we embrace with a kiss.
We step into a new, vibrant life,
with wisdom blooming in our spirits' light.
We celebrate this stage with pure delight.
Happy in our journey
with menopause,
our guide,
We bloom with grace and a fierce pride.

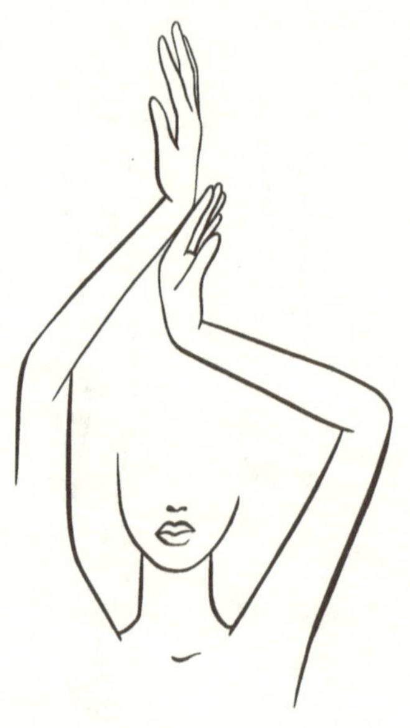

Season of Rain

Menopause arrives,
a season of rain.
Yet
within us,
joy and happiness remain.
No longer bound by monthly strife,
We celebrate our newfound freedom in life.
Embracing hot flashes,
sleepless nights,
we dance with passion;
our spirits take flight.
Menopause,
a journey of liberation and glee.
We embrace the beauty of being free.

Life's Rhythm

Life's rhythm shifts, a gentle ebb and flow.
Menopause arrives, a season to bestow.
A transition embraced, a woman's sacred gate,
a chapter closes, while another awaits.

Hormones dance, a symphony of change,
Hot flashes flicker, and emotions rearrange.
Yet amid the waves, a newfound power grows,
menopause, a rebirth, life's essence shows.

Wisdom deepens, like roots in fertile ground,
a metamorphosis where strength is found.
In this dance of life, menopause we embrace,
a journey of grace in this sacred space.

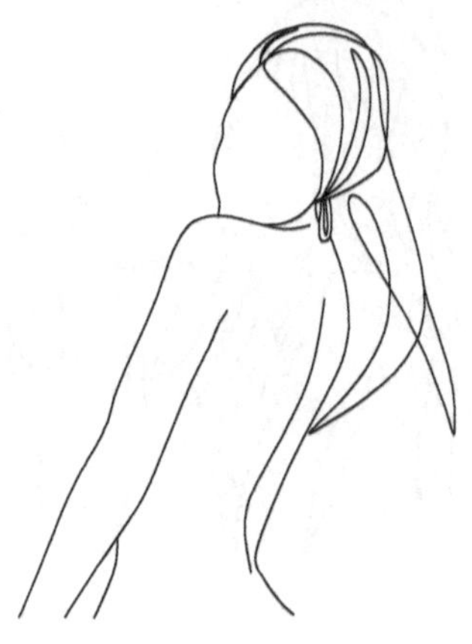

The Tapestry of Life

Life's tapestry weaves its intricate design.
Within its threads, menopause does align.
A transition, a chapter, a turning page,
where age meets wisdom, a seasoned sage.

Hot flashes and changes, body and mind,
menopause's dance, a rhythm defined.
Embracing the shift, with resilience we cope,
for in this journey, we find strength and hope.

A new phase unfolds, vibrant and true,
life's menopause, a rebirth we pursue.

Midlife Women Unite

Midlife women unite in this sacred phase
Menopause, where our power is ablaze
No longer defined by age or stage,
we break free from society's cage.

Together, we navigate uncharted seas,
Sharing stories and laughter with quiet ease.
Through hot flashes and night sweats, we find
a sisterhood bound, forever intertwined.

Embracing the change, we stand tall and strong.
United, we rise, a harmonious song.

Midlife Blossoming

Midlife, a time of blossoming anew,
where dreams and passions come into view.
In this chapter, we find our stride,
embracing the journey with joy and pride.

Wisdom gained from youthful days,
guides us through life's winding maze.
Midlife, a phase of self-discovery,
where we embrace our truest identity.

Midlife's Crossroads

Midlife's crossroads,
a moment of reflection,
where dreams and reality seek connection.
Navigating transitions,
uncertainties arise.
Seeking purpose,
as time swiftly flies.
In the depths of self-discovery,
we find
a new perspective,
a shift of the mind.
Midlife's Symphony,
an opportunity to grow,
embracing the journey,
letting our true selves show.

The Pure Dance of Midlife

Midlife brings a dance of pure delight,
a time to embrace joy with all our might.

We shed our worries, let our spirits soar,
midlife fun, a symphony to explore.

Adventures beckon, dreams come alive,
rediscovering passions as we strive.

Midlife, a chapter of laughter and glee,
where we embrace life and truly feel free.

I'm Going Crazy

I think I'm going crazy;
I think I'm losing my mind.
Why can't these thoughts stop coming?
The answer's hard to find.

I Am a Flame

I am a flame that burns so bright;
I am a flame that does not turn off at night.
I am a flame that has amazing powers;
I am a flame that roars for hours.
You can try to put me out;
you can scream, and you can shout.
But my flame will keep on burning bright
until the wee hours of the darkest night.

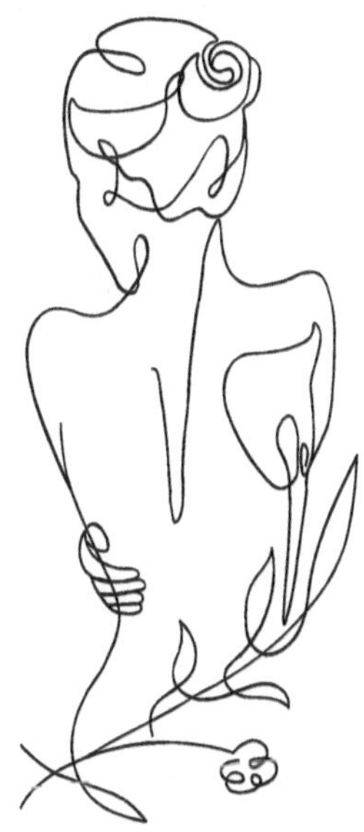

I Am Worthy

I worshiped you; I gave you my love.
I gave you everything I couldn't; I did.
I was bullied, not appreciated
I was not happy, not at peace
I was a punching bag, your fool.
Do not hurt me anymore; do not yell.
Do not call me names;
do not make me feel inferior.
For I am a human being; I deserve respect.
For I am worthy, for I am who I am.
No one can take that away from me.

You Are Beautiful

You are beautiful.
You are like the sun.
You are beautiful.
You are a unique one.
You are beautiful. You are a queen.
You are beautiful inside out and in-between.
You are beautiful.
You have to admit . . .
You are beautiful, and that is it!

Like a Lotus Flower

Like a lotus flower, you will . . .
Believe in yourself, and you will . . .
Like a lotus flower, achieve the immeasurable.
Believe in yourself, and you will, like a lotus flower,
select novel surroundings.
Believe in yourself, and you will, like a lotus flower,
lessen difficulties associated with each resolution.
Believe in yourself, and you will, like a lotus flower,
make the tough seem meek.
Believe in yourself, and you will, like a lotus flower,
relish the magnificence of the earth's creations.
Believe in yourself, and you will, like a lotus flower,
rise beyond your wildest expectations.
Believe in yourself, and you will, like a lotus flower,
discover talents hidden inside you.
Believe in yourself, and you will, like a lotus flower,
Be purified as you continue to be exceptional
and superior.
Believe in yourself, and you will, like a lotus flower,
acquire abilities and understanding from being.
Believe in yourself, and you will, like a lotus flower,
attain impossible dreams.
BELIEVE IN YOURSELF, like a lotus flower,
AND YOU WILL!

The Little Girl Inside Myself

There is a little girl who I see inside myself,
like the story in the novel, sitting on the shelf.
The little girl becomes a woman, who is someone's wife,
and there begins the story, the story of my life.
It is a story of happiness, a story of pain,
a story of experience, experience to gain.
The story of my life is not an easy one to tell,
for it is a story like heaven but also of hell.
I do not mean to frighten you
I do not mean to scare you
I do not mean that my story is a total nightmare.
There are times of happiness;
there are times of cheer.
There are times when my life
to me is very dear.
Since my life is one
that was chosen just to be,
I will be happy with what I have,
even though it's not really me.
I cannot go on, for the novel is too long,
I must put it back on the shelf,
and remember that I'm strong.

I Am Aware

I am a being who is aware of my emotions,
yet not aware of my needed devotions.
My life to me is dear,
yet there is daily hesitation and fear.
I want to be free to live my life as well as can be.
I want to be loved; I want to be me.
Myself is all I have;
that is all I need to be.
I take a breath.
I let it out.
I sing.
I shout.

Let It Go

Let go of negativity and anxiety . . . Let it go.
Let go of muddled beliefs . . . of hesitation,
Misplaced thoughts or verses . . . Let them go.
Let go of wrong reason . . . Let it go.
Let go of dread and conclusions . . .
Let go of anticipation . . .
Just let them go.

Don't check the elements; don't investigate. Let it go.
Don't say a word, no one will acknowledge or notice . . .
Like foliage tumbling from a tree . . . Let it go.
Don't promise, broadcast . . . Let it go.
It wasn't worth it; it wasn't wanted . . .
It was what it was, and is just that . . .
place a grin on your façade,
and forevermore,

JUST LET IT GO!

Yoga and Meditation

Yoga and meditation
fill my heart and soul.
They are the things that
make me feel most whole.

Yoga and meditation
are very dear to me.
Yoga and meditation
make my mind and body free.

I Am Me

I am not you; I am me.
I am worthy. I feel free.
I am happy. I am joyful.
I am proud, and I am soulful.
I am not my past. I am not my future.
I am the present.
I am who I was meant to be!

You Should

You should not fear,
for fear is fruitless.
You should not dread,
for dread never transpires.
You should not panic,
for panic is insignificant.
You should not borrow other people's problems,
for other's problems clutter your happiness.
You should not let others bring you down,
for it interferes with positive thoughts.
You should sleep with a clear mind,
for a clear mind makes a noble bedfellow.
You should restore the past, whether good or ill,
before it is gone forever.
You should count your blessings,
for they can vanish before your eyes.
You should listen, for only when you listen
do you hear.
Most of all,
you should appreciate YOU.

My Future Is the Present

My life to me is very dear,
yet there is hesitation and fear.
I want to be loved;
I want to be free.
Most of all, I want to be me.
I cry, I shout,
I take a breath.
I let it out.
I am a woman;
I am free.
My future
is a present to me!

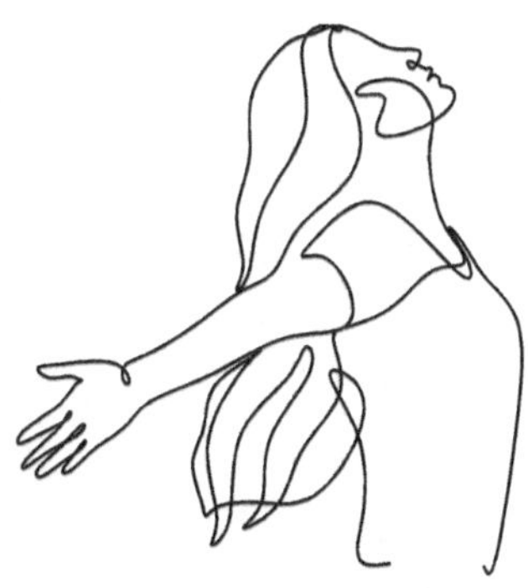

The Lonely One

Staring in the mirror,
gazing at my face . . .
why am I in this lonely place?
Can anybody hear me;
is anybody here?
I'm crying deep inside,
screaming from fear.

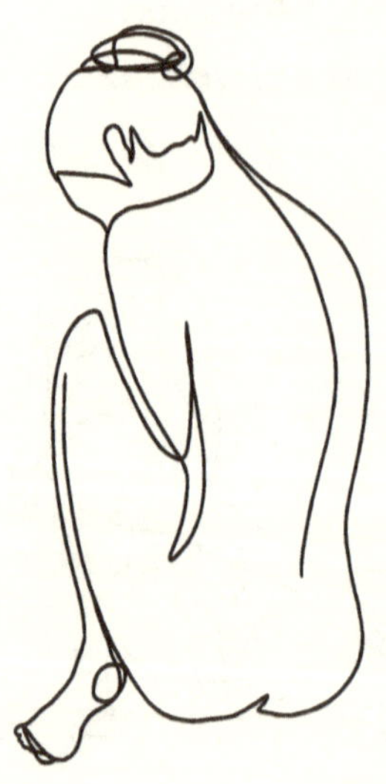

I'm Not Afraid

I'm not afraid of sorrow
I'm not afraid of pain

I'm not afraid of happiness
I'm not afraid of shame

I'm not afraid of people
I'm not afraid of change

I'm not afraid of the ocean
I'm not afraid of the sea

I'm not afraid of you
But I am afraid of me.

I Love You So Much

I love you so much, yet I feel so much hurt.
I don't know if you love me . . .
or her.

39

I Slumber in the Sky

I slumber and stare at the sky
I dream in clouds as I pray and cry
I endlessly dream as living passes me by

My dreams are real
They are what I feel

I dream of happy times, times without pain
times when my life wasn't insane
Why am I dreaming? Why am I here?
Why can't I float away into the atmosphere?

I'll never wake up
I'll never be me
I'll never know what could be

In my dreams, I have been here and there
In my dreams, I have been everywhere
I dream of riches. I dream of gold
I dream that my life in front of me will unfold
I cannot stay asleep forever.
For one day
I will wake up and say,
Good. I did not dream my life away.

The Stranger Inside Me

I feel a stranger lurking deep inside my mind,
yet this person is so hard to find.
She experiences tragedy; she experiences pain.
It really is a shame.

Why can't she be the person
who is not afraid of dark,
not afraid of light,
not afraid of people,
and not afraid to fight.

This stranger is a stranger that is stranger than them all.
Every time I see her, she is stranger than before.
Why can't she go away?
I pray, I pray, I pray.

She doesn't listen, but I feel she is here,
all throughout eternity, seasons, and years.

I have to learn to love her, because she will never die.
You see, she is not she,
for she is I.

The Little Girl

There was a little girl in my life,
so beautiful and smart,
I loved her with all my heart.

There was a little girl in my life,
her mother took her away from me
because of pride and dignity.

There was a little girl in my life,
with such a pretty face,
always dressed in pink bows and lace.

There was a little girl in my life, but she is no more,
now the little girl lives
behind someone else's door.

A Daughter's Fears

My darling little daughter,
with your eyes so bright,
why are you looking at me
with so much fright?

Don't be afraid of the world
I will teach you to fight!

You will be a little soldier
in a big world of tragedy and plight!

I will make you strong and able to see the rainbow's light.
You will see that the world can indeed be beautiful and white,
. . . not only black as night!

A Strong Daughter

My darling baby is two
What shall I say?
What shall I do?

I'll give you a party
Make food that is hearty

So you can grow strong
like a tiger in the zoo.

Moments I Breathe

Breathe
Some moments I feel strong
In the company of my true love.
Breathe
Some moments I feel rich
with my loving family.
Breathe
My love comforts and reassures me
just as my body is elevated by my façade.
Breathe
There is endless space in my heart and soul,
space for irrationality, which may come my way.
Breathe
I stand on a street corner and turn right;
I wonder what would happen if I turned left.
Breathe
I gaze at my true love
and remember all I treasured
our love, our beliefs, our thoughts
our way of life
until nothing was left
but a flickering candlelight
that did not blow out in the wind.
For that true love
lies deep within my heart.

I Love You More Than . . .

I love you more than words
I love you more than the birds
I love you more than the sky

I love you forever

I love you to the sun
I love you because you are fun
I love you more than words can say

I love you all day.

You

You are Proud.
You are Strong.
You are Right.
You are not Wrong.
You are You.
You are Unique.
You are Content, yet Meek.
You are You.
You are True.
You are not me.
You are You.

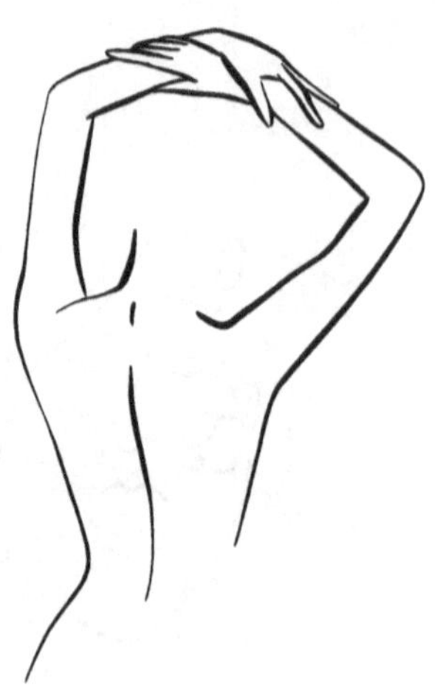

The Lady

The lady is crying
What did she do?

She looked in the mirror

She began to cry
Why is she so sad?

I wonder why?

Hello

Hello sunshine.
Hello rain.
Hello craziness.
I feel like I'm going insane.

Hello happiness.
Hello joy.
Hello pain.
Will the sun come out again?

Some Days

Some days,
I climb mountains
Some days,
I climb hills
Some days,
I simply stand still.

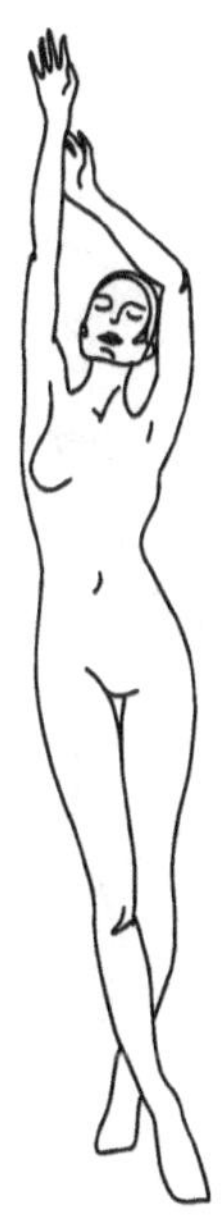

Menopause Days of the Week

Blue Mondays,
Tough Tuesdays,
Weird Wednesdays,
Thought-provoking Thursdays,
Freaky Fridays,
Soothing Saturdays,
Scary Sundays,
Those are my days of the week.

Suffering in Silence

Suffering in silence
I sit here by myself.
Suffering in silence
In such a lonely place.

Time

Time is coming
Time is here.

Time never stops
Neither does fear.

Why do I feel this way?
Every hour, every day?

Maybe life will get better next year.

A Beauty in Disguise

I am a beauty in disguise,
I see things through my eyes,
My world is upside down
I see things that make me drown.

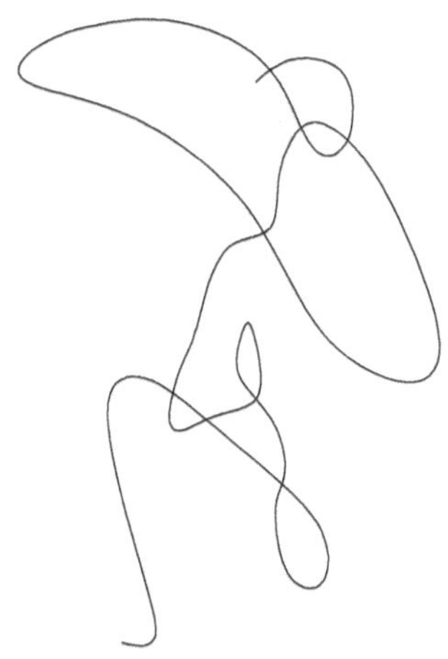

Distortion

My mind is not in proportion
I see myself in distortion.
Every day I am a different size
As I look in the mirror
with despise.
I see things that are not there
Why can't I be
fair?

Thoughts

Happy one day, sad the next,
These are the effects.

I feel great,
I feel bad,
I feel depressed—
The worst feeling I had.

The feeling doesn't disappear,
I wish it weren't here.

I take a breath and let it go.
Let it out to float away,
Allowing only good thoughts
to come my way.

Tea for You

Drink some tea, you will feel better.
Plunge in the sea, without your sweater.

Sit in the sun and have some fun.
Dance in the rain, let go of your pain.

Take a drink, it's time to think.
What will you do?
What will you say?

Let this happy feeling stay.

My Mind

My mind is wondering all day long,
I wish it would just sing me a song.

My mind wanders and wanders today.
I want it to stop.
It won't go away.

Why is my mind so much stronger than me?
Why can't I stop my thoughts from floating so free?

I close my eyes and try to dream deep.
I lessen the thoughts by counting sheep.

Yet my mind keeps wandering
miscellaneously,
I sigh and breathe,
and lay down my head,
as I gently float in my bed.

Sunshine in the Shadows of Darkness

The sun is shining.
The sky is clear.
Why is my head pounding with fear?
I don't know what is happening to me,
I don't know anything you see.
I want this feeling to leave,
I want to be happy again—relieved.
I want the sun to shine on me.
Let me feel free.
Let me be the woman,
I deserve to be.
Take away the shadows,
Take away the rain,
Take away my pain.

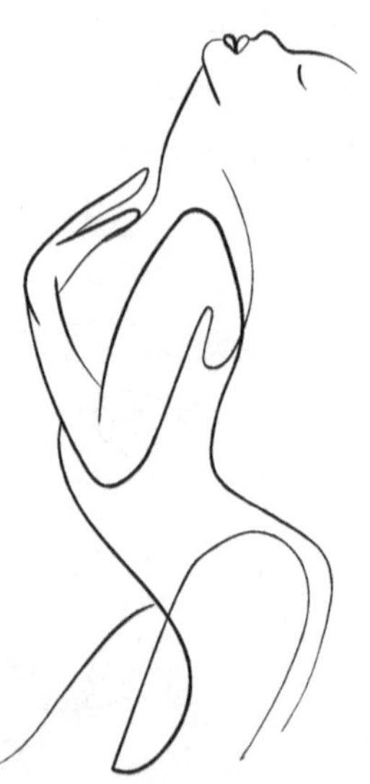

Self-Disillusion

I am resentful of the attention you give others
Why can't you give that to me?
Is it because I feel unhappy?
Is it because you want to feel free?
Is it in my mind?
The answer I cannot find.
Is it these years?
Or my fears?
I want to love my body
I want to be happy with me
I try to stay positive
but I cannot see.
I uncover my eyes
and look again
to see the person I was then.

Little Girl Gone

There is a little girl I used to be
Now this little girl I cannot see
I cannot see her smile
I cannot see her face
I want to be her in this scary place.
Where is this girl who I used to be?
When did she go away and leave me?
Come back, little girl
I need you here
Come back and take away my fear
Come back and help me smile
Come back and let me sing
I need to be you now
instead of me today.
I pray you hear me
and you come to stay.

It's a Hard Life

No one understands the life I lead
No one helps me when I am in need

No one is there when my thoughts come racing
No one sees what I am facing

I am alone in this lonely race
I hide the feelings from my face

Everyone thinks I am okay
When I tell them the truth, they are in dismay

Some days I can't hide it
Some days it is hard
Some days in silence, I fall apart.

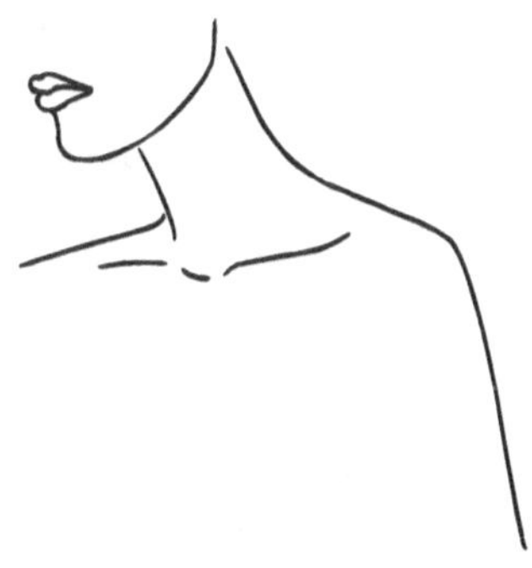

Deep Dark Thoughts

What makes me happy?
I cannot say.
What helps me find happiness
in my day?

My thoughts are deep
and dark in my mind.
Happiness, for me,
is not easy to find.

I go to my bed,
and lay myself down
as soon as my smile
turns into a frown.

Closing my eyes,
I think of good things and dream that
happiness lies upon my wings.

Feelings

Deep dark thoughts
scattered in my head.
Sometimes I think
I would be better off dead.

As I rub my tears away,
I begin to pray.

My mind is a jungle
with all kinds of thoughts
floating around
toward nothing ahead.

I shake my head;
the tears drift away,
and feelings of happiness
begin coming my way.

Why

Why is this happening to me?

Why is this the life I see?
Why can't I see beauty?

Why do I always see pain?
Why is every day the same?

Is it because of you?
Or is it because of me?

Why is this happening to me?

I Am a Woman

I am a woman who is proud.
I am a woman who is not loud.

I am a woman who is shy.
I am a woman, that is why.

I am a woman who is sad.
I am a woman who gets mad.

I am a woman who is meek.
Find me.
I am the woman that you seek.

I Am Lonely

I am lonely, yet I am not alone.
I am with you in this home.

I am quiet, yet I am speaking.
I am laughing, yet I am freaking..

I am nice, yet I am mean.
I am just blowing off steam.

Don't Fret the Small Things

Small things are minor,
yet they are HUGE.

Small things can clutter
the brain with refuge.

Don't fret the small things
because you deserve more.

Sweep them under the rug
and give yourself a hug.

Life Is Like a Poem

Life is like a poem,
a short story to be told.

Life has good times.
Life has bad times.
Life has sad times.

They are meant to be.
They are not wrong.

During our life,
we need to be brave
and strong.

Life Is Like Candy

Life is like candy
So sweet and delicious
Yet when we live it
the sweets can turn sour.

We need to focus
and use our breath for power.

The Sun Is Shining

The sun is shining.
The sky is blue.,

Yet I see clouds rolling by.

The wind blows,
clearing the clouds,
helping to keep
the sun in the sky.

The Power of Self-Love

Self-love is a powerful key
Guiding you through
every degree.
Without self-love
we cannot survive.
Self-love,
the ultimate guide.

Midlife Blues

I sing a sad song and cry.
I hide away because I am shy.

My face is not my own.
My body I disown.

Who is staring in the mirror
looking at me?

I do not recognize her.
Is it myself I see?

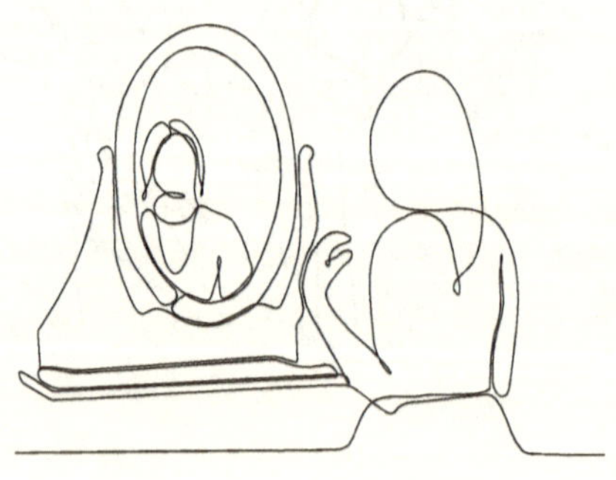

Lovely Lady

Lovely lady sitting in the rocking chair,
you have a lovely face,
lovely skin, a lovely body,
and lovely hair.

Why didn't I see this
when life was there?
Why did it take
until I sat in this chair?

I cannot cry about it now.
I should not care.

I will see your lovely features
until the day they are not there.

The Girl with a Beautiful Smile

There is a girl with a beautiful smile.
When she got older,
I looked for her for miles

I could not find her.

She disappeared one day.
Without warning, she went away.

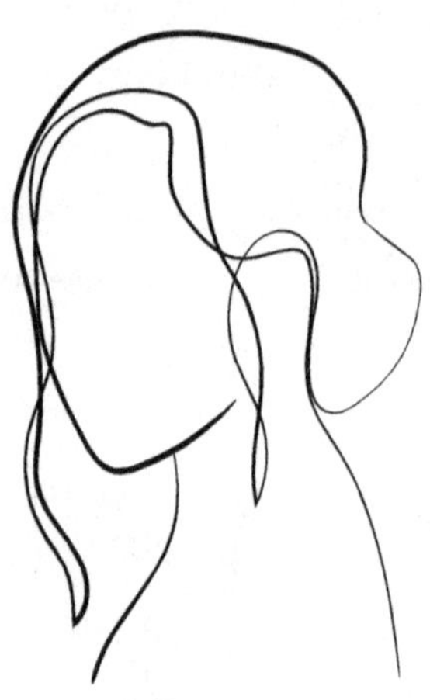

I Am a Flower

I am a colorful flower in a field of green grass.
I am a colorful flower full of beauty and sass.

I am a flower that blooms each year.
I am a flower that is bright,
not dull and gray.

I am
a colorful flower,
that's why
I am happy
each day.

Slippery Midlife

Midlife can be slippery.
Midlife can be tough.

It's all about your mindset
and how you take in stuff.

Wake up with a smile,
and you will see
that midlife can be
smooth as can be.

Looking Out the Window

Looking out the window
Looking out from in

I see the light.
I see the sky.
I see the sun.
I see the trees.

I see birds.
I see bees.
I see the grass.

I feel the warmth behind the glass.

Sweat Out the Small Stuff

I sit here, and a flush comes over me.
I sweat, yet I feel free.

I peel the clothes off my back.

I deserve to be comfortable.
I deserve to be me.

I should not care what people see.

I Love My Body

I love my body
It is a gift.

I love my body
I shall keep it healthy
and fit.

I love my body
I am thankful for it.

I love my body
it was given to me.

I love my body from now
until eternity.

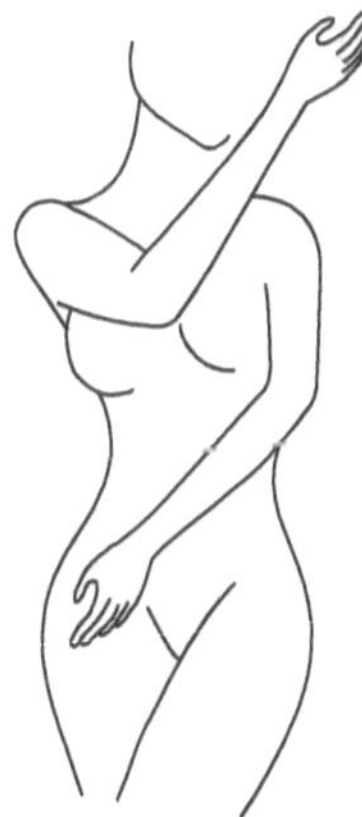

The Journey Called Life

Life is a journey
full of happiness and sorrow.
Just when it heads downhill,
it goes back up.

Just when it is hard,
it becomes easier than before.

Life is a journey that we all must take.
Live your life to the fullest,
even though it's not a piece of cake.

Life Is Like a Roller Coaster

Like a roller coaster we ride,
the life we were given with pride.

We go up; we go down,
sometimes we even go around
and upside down.

The thrill of life is not boring,
yet at times it appears
without a single warning.

Just when its scary,
it becomes calm.

So enjoy the ride
before it is gone.

No One Hears Me

No one hears me when I speak
I am quiet, I am meek.

No one hears me when I speak
Is my voice that weak?

No one hears me when I cry
Why am I so shy?

I feel like I am invisible.

I feel like I am not here.

I feel like I evaporated,
into the atmosphere.

I Am

I am me.
I am free.
I am happy.
Life is not crappy.
I am me.
Let me be.

Like the Wind

I feel like the wind
I wish I could fly

I wish I could reach the sky.

I feel like the wind
Please take me away

I want to be higher each day.

I want to be happy
I want to be me

Most of all,
I want to be free.

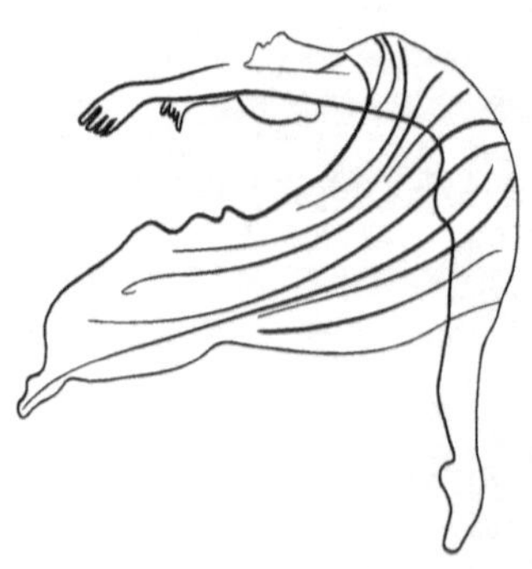

Breathe It Away

Take a breath
Let it all in

Let the breath
make our life begin

Our breath is a gift
we should all use

To give our bodies
an energy boost.

Protect Me

A man should protect his woman.
She trusts him to defend her life.

The weak man is not a man
if he isn't kind to his wife.

A woman deserves more than a home.

She deserves a protected life,
knowing she is not alone

I Know Who You Are

When I met you, you were just a boy.
I thought you'd give me happiness and joy.

I fell for your lies until it became clear,
You were a wolf disguised as a deer.

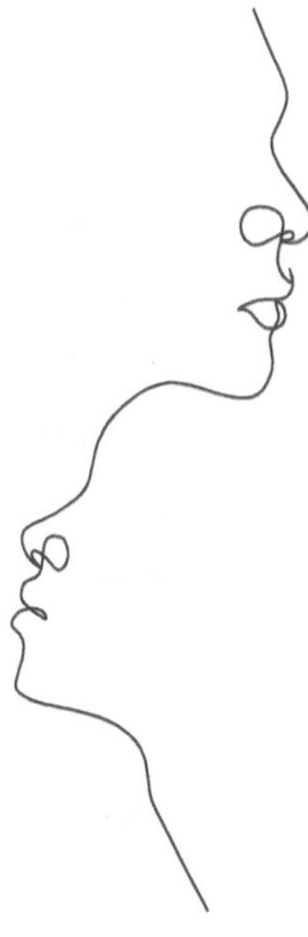

Beauty Lies in the Eyes

Beauty is only skin deep,
my innocence is for me to keep.

I don't want you near.
Stay away from me.

My life is too dear.
Your message is clear.

We are not meant to be.
That is what I see.

I don't like you.
I don't care.
I don't know.
I can't think.
Leave me alone.
Go away.
Do not stay.

Lemons and Flowers

When life gives you lemons,
squeeze out all the juice.

Look at the flowers,
as a sign of your youth.

Youth is but a frame of mind.
It comes and goes,
with each thought,
with each breath,
with each word.

Unless the word is unkind

You Are but a Dot

You are but a dot
You are but a spot

This world is big
you melt into it

No one sees you
No one cares

Take a chance
show your colors

Bloom with the flowers
Enjoy the years,
months,
and hours.

For life is short
It melts away
faster and faster
with each day.

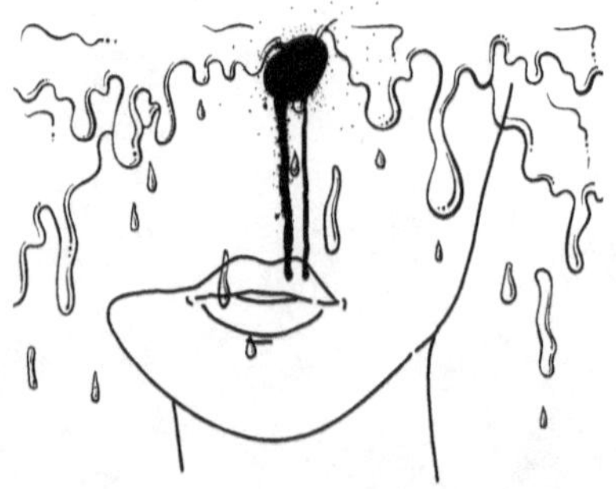

91

Me, Myself, and No One Else

I have no one to talk to
No one to share with

No one cares.

I am alone
I am scared

I have to learn
to love myself.
To trust myself.

I don't need anyone,
because,
I have me.

Give Me Your Hand

Give me your hand.
Give me your breath.
Give me your soul.

Give me your words.

Guide me gently.
I appreciate you.
Love me always,
and I will love you.

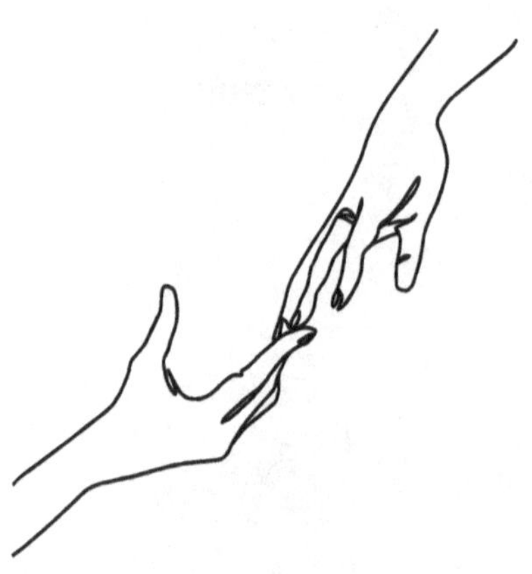

Cotton Candy Clouds

I stare at the blue sky.
I stare at the clouds floating by.
Like clean cotton candy
above my head.

I feel the sweetness of the white color,
like a purity I once knew.

Let me go back and return to that place.
The place of innocence in this corrupt human race.

The Willow Tree

In my dream,
I passed by a willow tree one gloomy day.

The wind began to blow.
The branches began to sway.
The stream began to flow.

I was walking by a willow tree on a sunny day.

The sun began to shine.
The branches were still.
There was a trickle in the stream.

And at that moment,
I knew my life
was more than just a dream.

The SAD Woman

The SAD Woman sits alone.
The SAD Woman counts her prayers.
The SAD Woman walks down the stairs.

Down into the abyss.
Nothing gives her happiness.

The Sad Woman turns her head.
The SAD woman is DEAD.

Out comes the blissful one.
Out comes the SUN.

Butterflies

Butterflies are like bees
gliding up along the breeze

Butterflies don't make a sound
butterflies glide above the ground

Butterflies have wings that soar
I bet inside them is a roar.

Birds Sing

The birds sing all day long
sing some happy and sad songs

Are they happy all the time?
Are they singing us a rhyme?

Why do birds sing when in a tree?
Why can't I be like a bird
and feel free?

Midlife

When we get older, we get wise.
When we get older,
we shouldn't have to disguise.

When we get older, life gets good.
When we get older, I heard it should.

When we get older, as does everyone.
When we get older, we should have more fun.

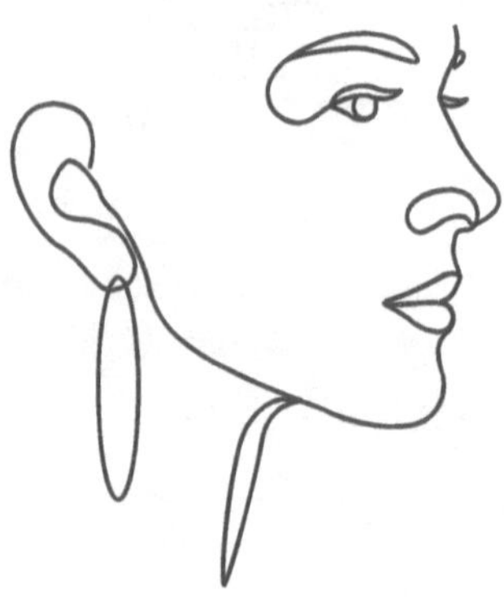

The Voice in My Head

There is a voice
I hear inside my head
It's there at night
It won't let me get to bed

This voice keeps chattering
as my thoughts keep gathering

I toss and turn
and shake my head

Let this voice go away
I want to sleep
but instead I pray.

I Do

I do as I'm told
Not as I say

I do it for you
I do it for them

I should do it for me
and not listen again.

Thoughts

Thoughts are running through my head.
I wonder where they came from
as I lie in my bed.

The thoughts are running
like water in a stream.

I am so tired
I want to dream.

The Alley Cat

The alley cat preys on its feed
Just like you prey on me.

The house is quiet as can be.
The mouse is timid
as you can see.

The alley cat is fierce yet gentle as well.
The alley cat is me—
can you tell?

Happiness

Happiness is hard to find.

Inhale and exhale,
just like the wind.

The clouds roll by.

The sun shines on the trees.

Happiness is easy to find.
Just leave negativity behind.

A Joyful Transition

Menopause arrives,
a joyful transition.
Embracing change,
with hearts full of elation.
No longer bound
by monthly strife,
We embrace freedom,
embracing life.
With newfound wisdom,
we stand tall,
Happy in the journey,
embracing it all.

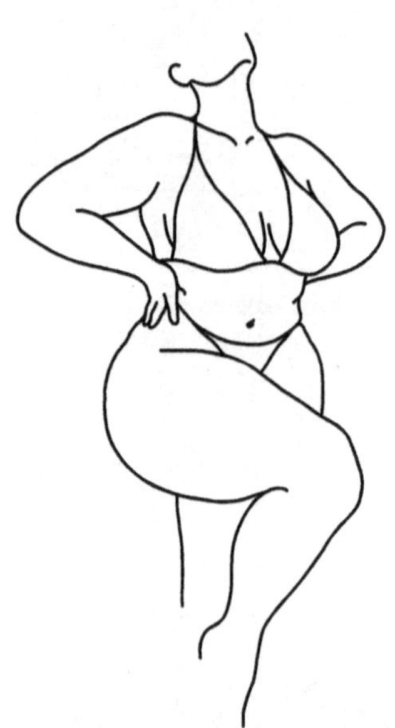

Dark Lady

Dark lady standing in the sun
Dark lady, try to have some fun

Dark lady, why are you so blue?

Dark lady, try to see the light

Dark lady, don't be sad
Dark lady, it's not so bad.

Circle of Life

Little girl why are you so cheerful?
Little lady starting to get fearful
Little woman not having a ball
Older lady taken a fall.

Little woman not caring anymore
Little lady passing by the sun
Little girl, why are you a lonely one?

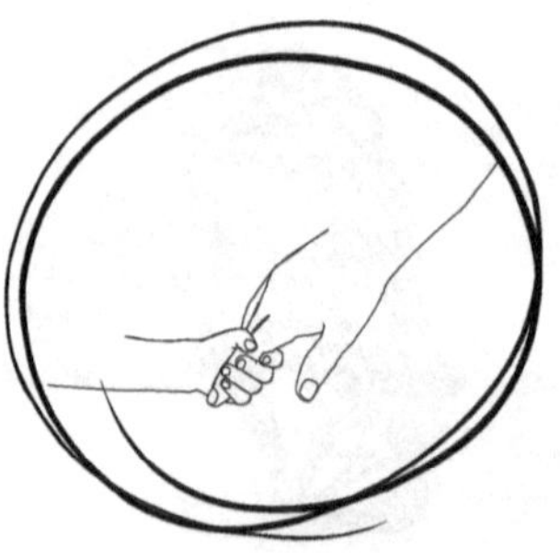

Time

Time can be an enemy.
Time can be your foe.

Time can go fast.
Time can go slow.

The clock is ticking faster each day.
Don't let time
take the woman you are away.

Flowers

The flowers are blooming
So are you

Look in the mirror
Look at your face

Look at the woman in that space

Look at the ocean
Look at the sea
Look at yourself
Don't look at me.

My Mind

My mind is a tool I can use to feel good.
My mind can let me be understood.

My mind was given to me as a gift.
My mind is always there when I need a lift.

My mind allows me to think,
yet it can also make me sink.

Life

Life is happy
Life is sad

Life is good
Life is bad

Life is energy
Life is free

Life is for you and for me.

Let's live the life we desire
because before we know it,
it will be out—
like watering a fire.

I Am Not Feeling It

I am not feeling it today.
I am not well.
Get me out of this darkness,
the one called hell.

I have not sinned;
I have not cried.
So why do I feel
like the woman I once knew
has died?

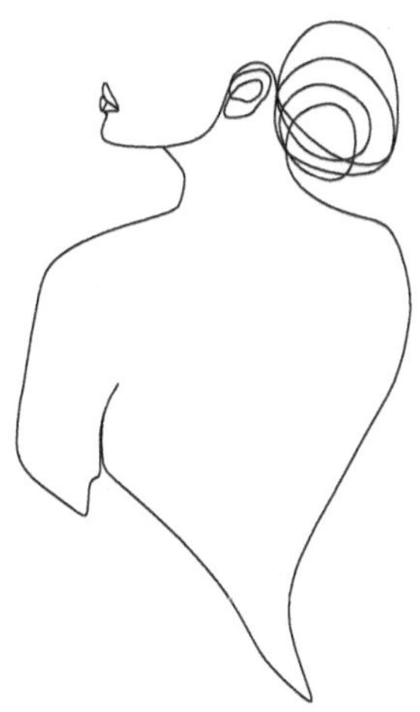

Happiness Is Pain

If happiness is heaven,
Why do I only feel pain?

If happiness is a good thing,
Why does it feel bad?

If happiness is supposed to make me happy
Why do I always feel sad?

I Am Floating

I feel like I am floating
I feel like I am not here

I feel like this is a dream
Like I'm floating in a stream

It's hard to be me.
It's hard to fit in society.

I try,
but at this age,
it's not my priority.

My Twisted Mind

My mind is twisted,
or so they say.

My mind is not like everyone else's.

This happened to me,
just the other day.

I woke up as someone I did not know,
I woke up feeling scared of my own shadow.

Birds Fly

Birds are flying
The sky is blue

Why am I not the person I once knew?
I ask this question with no answer.

The seconds are ticking
The minutes are clicking
The hours are tracking
The days are cracking

The weeks are going
The months are showing
The years are flying
Yet I'm still here trying.

Bleeding Heart

My heart is bleeding for you.
My heart is broken in two.

My heart is aching.
My heart is breaking.

The pain is too much to bear.
I love you.
Why don't you care?

My Life in a Nutshell

My life, in a nutshell, is hard to crack.
My life to me became a hack.
I have ups, and I have downs.
I have good days and bad days.
Overall,
I feel happy,
. . . except when I fall.

Today

Today is here
Soon it will be gone

Tomorrow is coming
Time is running

Life is short
Live to the fullest
whenever you can
Or it will pass you by
like the clock that is ticking
like the wind in the sky.

The Voice in My Head

I hear a voice deep inside my head.
It told me something,
but I am not sure what it said.

The voice keeps getting louder,
yet I cannot really hear it.

I know its there;
maybe the problem is I fear it.

I Look in the Mirror

I look in the mirror and see
an old, sad woman staring at me.

She looks weary,
yet she smiles.

She has experience.
She has wisdom.

Who is this old woman?
For I do not know.

I look again,
and to my surprise,
I see myself in her eyes.

My Heart

I feel my heart beating
faster and faster.

I feel the love in your laughter.

I know you love me,
but I do not love myself.

For I am not happy;
I don't know why.

I wish I could float,
away in the sky.

Tears of Sadness

I hold back my tears of my sadness.

I hold back my screams of madness.

I hold back my sorrow.

I hold back my joy.

I hold back my life.

My dreams I destroy.

Living Is Not for ME

Living should be easy.
Living should be fun.
Living should be a pleasure
for everyone.

Living is for you,
yet it is not for me.

I tried living one time
and did not feel free.

My Body

My body took on a new façade,
it must have been an act of God.

My body is not my own,
I do not recognize it when I'm alone.

I must remember that my body is my home.

It will always be with me,
no matter where I roam.

I will learn to love my body,
just the way it is,
accept it like a gentle kiss.

Midlife Woman

Midlife woman,
you are in your prime,
with wisdom and grace,
you shine.
You have lived and learned.
Grown and changed, yet through it all,
you have remained untamed.
You have faced your fears
and taken risks;
you have learned to love yourself,
discovered your passions,
your dreams,
and now are living to the extreme.

Resilient Midlife Woman

You are a midlife woman
You are strong and resilient
You are wise and kind
You are a force to be reckoned with,
no one can deny it.

You have earned your stripes
and paid your dues.
Now you are ready for whatever life
has in store for you.

Dear Midlife Woman

Dear woman of midlife,
Your tears are not in vain.
It's normal to feel pain.

The weight of your choices
can be too much to bear.
The dreams you once had
may seem too distant to care.

The woman you've become is exactly
who you're meant to be.

Your scars and your struggles
have shaped you into gold.
Your wisdom and grace
are a treasure to behold.

A Time to Reflect

Midlife is a time to reflect.
To ponder joys and regrets.

A time to make amends with the past
Embrace your strengths
Acknowledge limitations
Enjoy life's simple pleasures with elation.

Midlife is a time to let go
of all the things that hold you back
A time to open your heart and soul
and follow a path you lack.

A time to connect with others.
Build relationships that matter most.
A time to find comfort,
and cherish the ones you hold close.

Life Is a Journey

Amid life's journey,
I found myself anew.
A woman with scars
but a heart that still knew
how to love and cherish
this person I've become.
A midlife woman,
proud and strong, no longer on the run.
I gaze into the mirror, and what do I see?
A woman with wrinkles and a smile that is free.

I embrace my flaws,
for they make me unique.
I love my strengths, for they allow me to speak.

I dance to my own beat.
I sing my own song.

For I am a midlife woman,
and I've found where I belong.

A Strong Midlife Woman

A midlife woman, wise and strong,
embraces self-love all day long.

She dances freely to her own beat,
and wears her heart upon her sleeve.

She laughs with joy and cries no shame,
for her self-love is her constant aim.

She finds peace in moments of stillness,
and practices self-care with the utmost will.

She feeds her soul with love and light,
and radiates a beauty that's oh-so bright.

For she knows that love begins within,
and within herself, she'll always win.

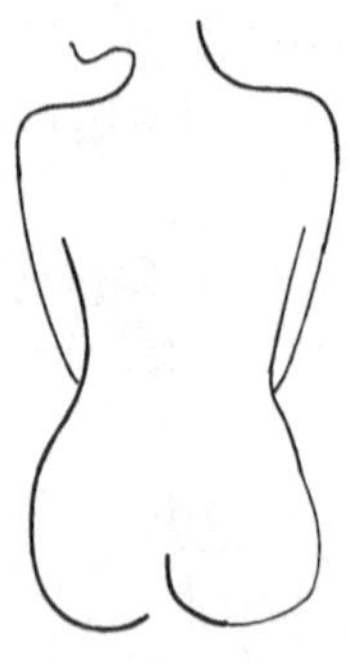

Love Yourself

In midlife, she learned to love herself
With confidence and grace
She found her wealth

No longer bound by others' expectations
She embraced her flaws and imperfections.

She looked in the mirror and saw beauty
No longer seeking validation or duty.

Her love for herself grew stronger each day
As she let go of the past and found her own way

She smiled at her reflection and said with glee,
"I am enough, and I love me!"

So, if you're a midlife woman feeling lost
remember
self-love comes at no cost,

Embrace who you are and all you can be
For the greatest love of all
is the one that sets you free.

A Season of Change

Midlife is a season of change and growth.
We look back on our past,
reflect on what we achieved,
and think about the things
we still want to receive.

It's a time to let go of what no longer serves.
To release old beliefs and self-imposed curves.
To embrace the present and all that it holds,
and step into our power, solid and bold.

We face challenges, but we are equipped
with the knowledge and skills we picked up along the way.

Midlife is a time to love ourselves more,
to appreciate the person we have become,
and to cherish each moment as it comes.
To live our lives with purpose, like charms,
to welcome this season with open arms.

For midlife is a gift, a chance to grow.
To become the best version of ourselves and glow.

The Youthful Glow

Oh dear, how the years have flown.
My once youthful glow is somewhat drawn.
The mirror shows a face with lines
and strands of grey in these locks of mine.
But wait, hold on, take a breath,
and think of all the joys that I've met.
The love I've shared,
the battles won.
The laughter, tears,
and songs I've sung.
I've raised my kids,
I've faced my fears
and even wiped my tears.
I've learned to love myself,
flaws and all.
I stood up tall
through it all.
So here's to me, the midlife queen
who has lived her life,
within all her means.

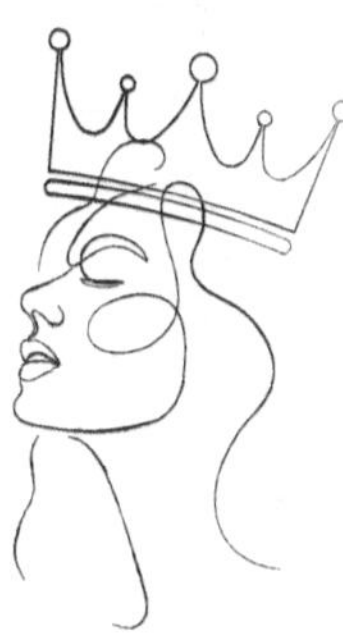

A Midlife Woman in Despair

A midlife woman in despair
lost without a care.
Searching for a sign,
something to bring peace of mind.
Because she is running out of time.
She looks back on her life
with disappointment
and strife.
All the hopes that she had
now seem so distant and sad,
but deep within her soul,
a spark begins to take control.
She knows she has the strength
to face her fears—
and go to any length.
She'll pick herself up and try
to live life before she dies.
She'll find the courage to believe
in herself and all she can achieve.

The Empty Room

She sits alone in her empty room
Amid a midlife gloom.
Her thoughts are heavy- her heart is sore.
She wonders what the future has in store.
She's lived her life the best she could,
but now she's lost and misunderstood.
Her dreams have faded- her spirit low.
She wonders where she'll find her flow.
The wrinkles on her face clearly show how
the years have come- and how they go.
She wishes she could turn back time,
to when life was simple,
and she was in her prime.

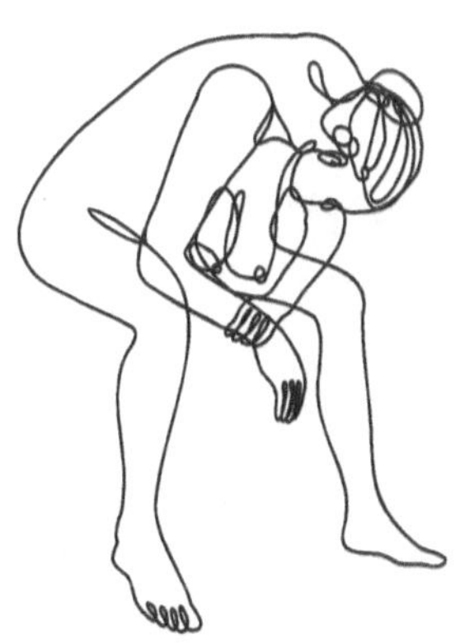

To My Younger Me

Oh, younger me, so full of hope and dreams,
your life ahead, so bright it seems.
But listen closely; let me share
words of wisdom from the future I bear.
Youthful beauty fades away,
but inner strength will always stay.
Chase your passions; live without fear.
Cherish every moment, my dear.
Life is short; make it count.
Don't waste time on petty doubt.
Embrace your flaws for
they make you unique.

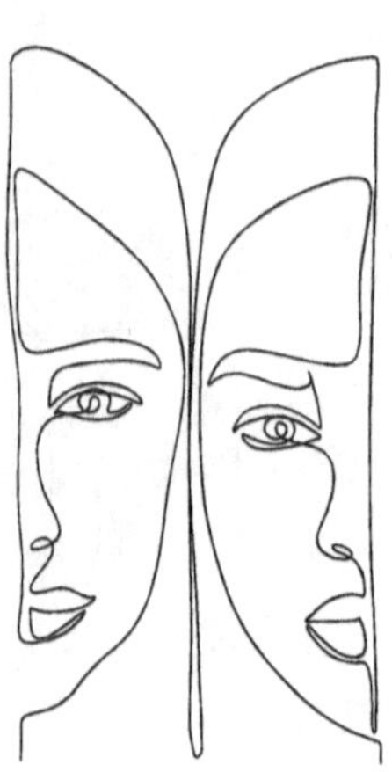

The Adventures Ahead

I've come too far to give up now.
I'll take a deep breath and a bow.
I've learned so much along the way.
I'll keep learning every day.
I've made mistakes,
but I've grown too.
I'll keep pushing until I'm through.
At times I feel like I've lost my way
and that the world has nothing left to say.

I'm stronger now than I've ever been,
I know that I'll rise again.
I'll face each challenge with grace and poise,
and celebrate all of life's little joys.

A New Beginning

Menopause, a chapter that is new,
A transformation, brave and true.
Through changes we find our way,
embracing life's vibrant display.

Hormones shift, emotions soar,
But strength and wisdom lie at our core.
In this journey, we stand tall,
embracing the beauty of it all.

Hot flashes come, then fade away,
navigating each passing day.
With grace and resilience, we emerge,
unveiling a spirit that will surge.

Menopause, a time to reflect,
to honor the woman we resurrect.
In this stage, we find our worth,
a celebration of our rebirth.

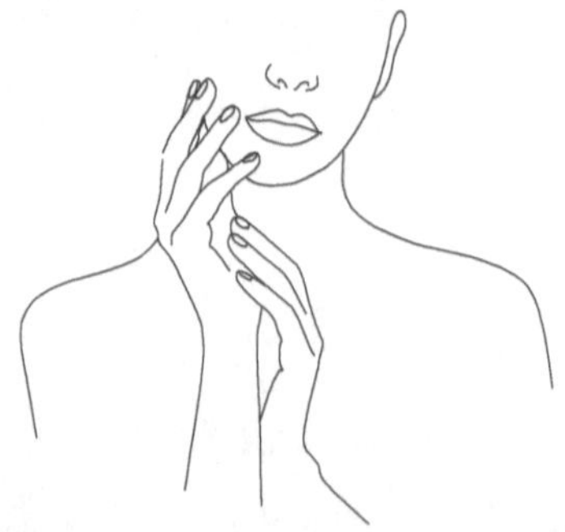

A Journey of Change

Menopause, a journey of change,
Embracing life's new, subtle range.
A chapter closing, another begun,
In this transformation, we find strength won.

Hot flashes flicker, emotions rise,
As wisdom deepens, our spirits fly.
With grace, we navigate this unknown,
Menopause, a bloom proudly grown.

So let us honor this sacred transition,
With self-care and love as our mission.
Menopause, a chapter bittersweet,
We embrace the change, our hearts replete.

A Time of Transformation

Menopause, a time of transformation,
From fertile youth to a new phase,
embrace the journey; embrace the grace.

Hot flashes come, then drift away.
Night sweats disrupt slumber's stay.
But amid it all, a strength emerges,
a phoenix rising, our soul converges.

No longer bound by cycles past,
we bloom anew, free at last.
Let's honor this time, embrace it whole,
a chapter of life bound to unfold.
Menopause a tapestry to be woven,
a woman's journey, forever unbroken.

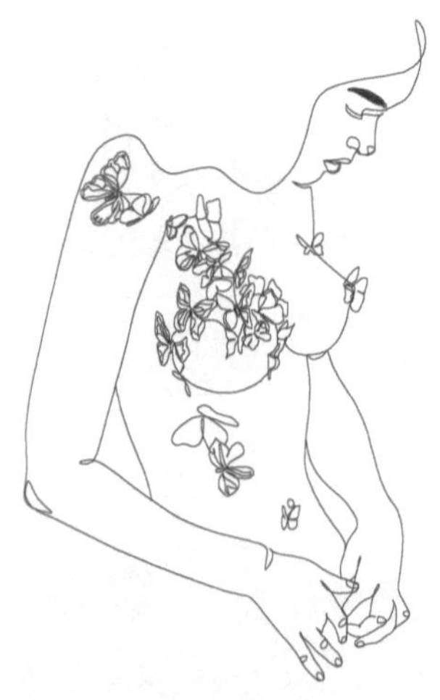

Graceful Menopause

Menopause, a journey of grace,
a transformation, a sacred space.

Through ups and downs, we find our way,
embracing new chapters, day by day.

Hormones shifting, emotions run high,
but our strength will never die.

Like a phoenix rising, we soar above,
with menopause a symbol of self-love.

No longer defined by youthful guise,
We embrace wisdom, where beauty lies.

Age and Wisdom

In the realm of age, where wisdom prevails
Midlife women gleam with stories and tales

Lines etched upon their faces, eternally wise
Each wrinkle a chapter, a truth that belies

With grace, they walk like queens of time
Old women, majestic, their spirits sublime

Through the years, they've weathered life's storms
Their beauty is unyielding, a true art form

In their presence, a symphony of strength and grace
midlife women, a testament to life's wondrous embrace

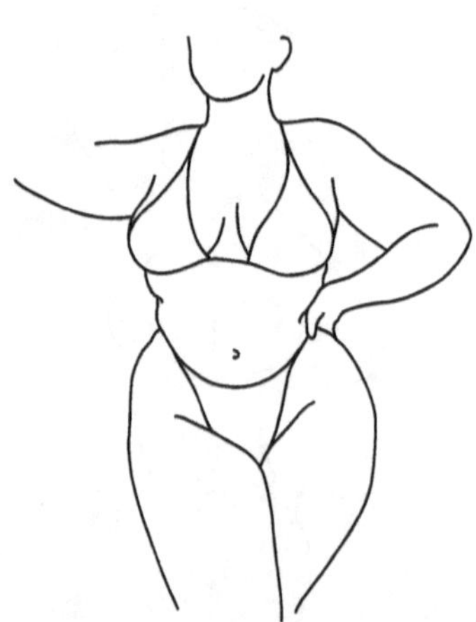

Midlife Women Warriors

Midlife women
Warriors at heart
Navigating life's challenges
Playing their part

With fire in their souls
They rise above
Harnessing strength
Fueled by dreams and love

They've weathered storms
And conquered fears
Wisdom and resilience
Etched through the years

With grace and tenacity
They face each day
Empowering others
And lighting the way

Midlife Women Unchained

Midlife women,
with spirits unchained
In the depths of their souls,
courage ignites
With unwavering hearts
they conquer new heights

Through trials and triumphs
they boldly stride
And from deep within
they hide
Challenges faced with unwavering grace
Midlife warriors whose
fierce determination they embrace

Souls on Fire

Midlife women,
with fire in their souls,
Navigate the challenges that life holds.
They stand tall and fearless
against the tide
Harnessing power,
they won't be denied.
With wisdom as armor,
they forge ahead
in pursuit of dreams,
no matter what is said.
They embrace their worth,
their voices resound.
Shattering barriers
and breaking new ground.

Midlife's Golden Embrace

In midlife's golden embrace,
women exude warmth and grace.
They radiate joy with every step,
embracing life's blessings while awake.
Hearts full of wisdom,
they find their bliss.
Embracing new adventures
with a joyful kiss.

With gratitude in their hearts,
they thrive,
Embracing the beauty of being alive.

The Realm of Midlife

In the realm of midlife, where happiness resides,
midlife women bloom, embracing joyful strides.
With hearts aglow, they cherish life's sweet gifts,
creating moments their spirits truly lift.

Their laughter echoes like a melody of cheer,
embracing passions,
making dreams crystal clear.

Through love and friendship,
their hearts are entwined,
radiating warmth, their presence is so kind.

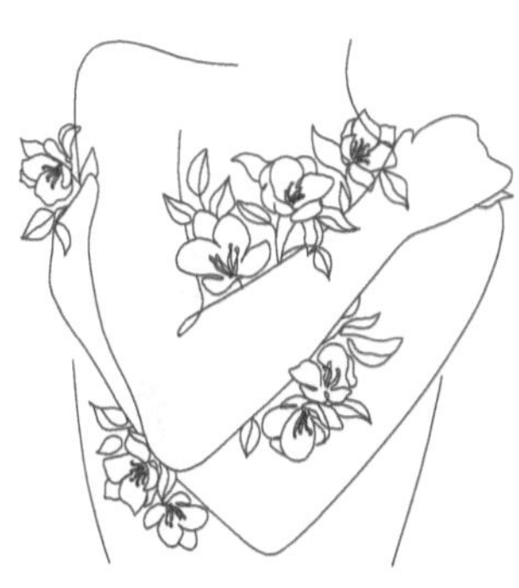

The Arrival of Menopause

Menopause arrives, a natural change
a journey embarked with courage in range
A metamorphosis, a transition profound
Where womanhood's essence continues to astound

Hormones shifting, like tides of the sea
A dance of emotions, a chance to be free

Hot flashes flicker, like flames burning bright
But within the heat, emerges renewed light

Embracing the wisdom that time has bestowed
Menopause, a chapter of strength overload

Midlife Bloating

In midlife, bloating may appear,
an unwelcome guest causing fear.
Do not fret for it shall pass,
like shadows waving in the grass.
Hormones fluctuate,
causing shifts within.
Water retention, a battle we can win.
Stay hydrated, nourish with care,
Choose healthy food,
and breathe clean air.
Engage in movement,
exercise to thrive.
In this journey,
your strength will revive.

The Weight of Menopause

Weight gain may arise
Hormones shift, metabolism is slow
With balance and care, your radiance will show.

Find joy in movement, dance and sway,
For in self-love's embrace, you'll find your way.

Menopause, a new chapter, not an end
Embrace's your body,
allowing your your spirit to transcend.

Nurture Thyself

Nurture thyself with mindful choices made,
Nourish with wisdom, let health cascade.

Embrace movement, let exercise be thy guide.
Build strength and resilience, side by side.
For menopause, though it may persist,
With patience and care, it can be dismissed.

Focus not on symptoms
but on feeling strong.
In this journey, you truly belong.
So love thyself fiercely
with body and soul.
Menopause's symptoms
shall not take their toll.

Midlife Beauty

In midlife's embrace,
beauty takes a new form
Radiating from within, a light that is warm.

Lines etched upon your face
like stories told
Each wrinkle a testament
a beauty to behold
With grace and wisdom
confidence unfurled
Midlife unveils a beauty that transcends the world.

The Power of Midlife

Midlife women,
strong and bright,
embracing wisdom's guiding light.
With grace they navigate life's maze.
With laughter, love,
and steadfast gaze.
They bloom anew,
like flowers fair,
with stories rich and hearts to share.
In every step,
a newfound power
Midlife's women,
strength is your power.

Midlife Women

Midlife women,
With grace they age,
Like fine wine,
Their spirits shine.

Through ups and downs,
They find their way,
Embracing life, come what may.

Like Stars in the Night

Like stars that twinkle in the night,
Midlife's women shine so bright.
With laughter's melody and vibrant hearts,
They conquer obstacles, playing their parts.

They're poets of life, crafting their verse,
Their stories woven, blessing the universe.
Embracing passions, dreams set free—
Midlife's women, radiant, carefree.

Vibrant Midlife Women

Midlife women, vibrant and strong,
They dance through life's rhythm,
singing along.
With grace and wisdom,
they navigate.
The challenges they face,
they confidently break.
Their spirits soar,
like birds in the sky—
Midlife women, fierce and spry.
They bloom anew,
like flowers in spring,
Embracing their power,
with every note they sing.

Midlife's Embrace

Midlife's embrace
is a woman's grace,
A tapestry woven
with wisdom's trace.
With hearts alight,
we conquer the night
Radiating strength,
a shimmering light.

Bold and sublime,
we bloom in our prime,
Navigating paths,
with rhythm and rhyme.

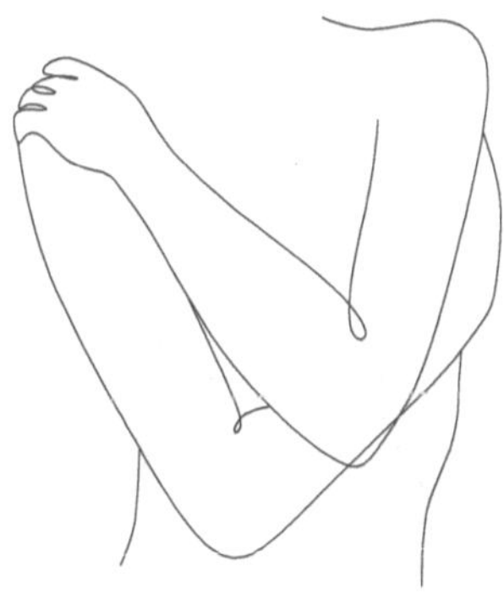

The Midlife Race

Within the midlife race
Women find grace
A symphony of strength
with hearts that brace
With wisdom's touch, spirits unfold
Radiating beauty, like stories untold
Dancing through challenges
with fires ablaze
Embracing self-worth
in myriad ways
Midlife women, a tapestry divine
brilliance shining
with love in golden shine.

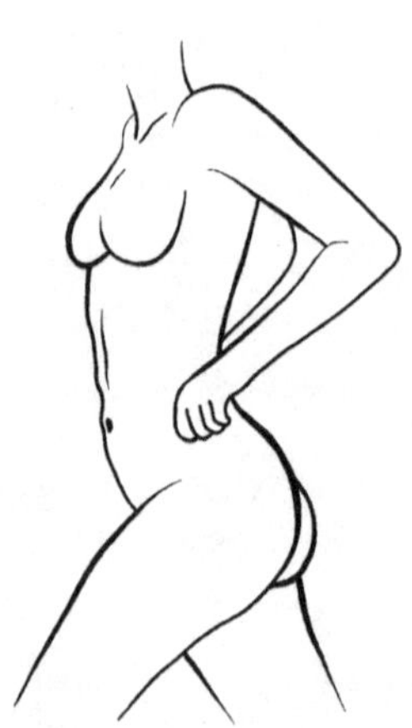

A Midlife Tale to Be Told

Amid midlife's grand tale
we stand
Midlife's women
bold and grand.
With grace and wisdom,
we navigate the years
Our laughter echoes
erasing fears
Embracing change
we bloom like flowers
Harnessing strength
our spirits never cower
Midlife women
vibrant and full of zest
Radiate brilliance
shining our best.

Midlife's Gloom

In midlife's gloom
we gracefully stride
Wisdom's crown adorns us with pride
Our spirits soar
unburdened and free
Midlife's women
embracing our destiny
With every step
our confidence beams
we chase our dreams
fulfilling our schemes

In strength we find,
our truest delight

Midlife's women,
we shine so bright

Golden Rays

Midlife's golden rays upon her face,
She dances through this joyous space.
Laughter bubbling from her soul,
Her spirit and body shine as a whole.
In midlife's embrace,
she finds her stride,
Embracing every moment,
far and wide.
Her heart, ablaze
with passions anew,
She paints her world a vibrant hue.

Midlife's Radiance

Midlife's sun shines on her radiant face
A time of joy to embrace
Wisdom gained
dreams held tight
Midlife woman basking in the light.
Dancing through life with vibrant grace
Embracing love and laughter
at a lively pace.
Each moment cherished,
each day anew
Midlife woman shine
your spirits true.

Midlife's Bloom

Amid life's vibrant tune
Midlife's joyous season begins to bloom
With hearts aflame
Embracing the years
Midlife women
Shed their fears
They dance with laughter
Their spirits high
Unleashing dreams
And reaching for the sky.

Shadows in the Midlife

Amid the shadows
Once obscured in the night
Midlife's women awaken
Basking in a newfound light.
Like a phoenix rising from ashes
They soar
Unveiling their essence
Radiating a little more.

With wisdom as their guide
They navigate their way
Embracing beauty
Each brand-new day.

Whispers

Within midlife's gentle whispers,
secrets are revealed
The power of self-love,
an eternal shield
Shedding layers of doubt
embracing self-worth

Midlife's women shine
as beacons on this Earth.

With hearts aglow
radiating pure grace

Seeing the light in midlife
finding a special place.

The Canvas of Midlife

Midlife,
a canvas where vibrant hues reside
where dreams bloom
and aspirations collide.
A time to shed inhibitions
and embrace the new
to explore passions
with courage, that's true.

Midlife,
a canvas where life begins
where living is cherished
and each heartbeat wins.
A time to savor, to love
and forgive
to embrace beauty in the life we live.

Midlife

Midlife
where life truly thrives
A time to embrace
feeling fully alive
No longer bound by youth's trends
Midlife
where authenticity begins.
Passions reignited
dreams take flight.
Midlife
a time to savor
and bask in delight.
Midlife
an essence,
a symphony well-led.
So seize the moment
let your spirit soar
Midlife
a time to live
forevermore.

The Season of Midlife

Midlife,
a season to live
When the heart whispers,
it's time to give.
Permission for dreams
that have long been suppressed
Soar on wings, no longer repressed.
A time to savor moments
with delight
Embracing passions,
igniting the light.

Gentle Whispers

Midlife's gentle whispers
Secrets revealed
Power of self-love
An eternal shield
Shedding layers of doubt
Embracing our worth
Midlife women shine
As messengers on earth.

Midlife's Dance

With graceful steps, we sway and spin,
Embracing the rhythm that stirs from within.

No longer confined by the boundaries of youth,
Midlife's stage becomes our stage of truth.

We move with confidence, in sync with our souls,
Expressing our essence as the music unfolds.

Each twirl and turn, a liberation so sweet,
In midlife's dance, we find freedom complete.

Midlife Rhythm

Midlife's rhythm
dancing through the years
our souls like prisms.

With grace and poise
we sway to life's tune
Midlife women,
our spirits in bloom.

With each step
we shed inhibitions
reveling in newfound
passions and ambitions.

With confidence and joy
our bodies sway to
midlife's rhythm,
a celebration every day.

A Gentle Embrace

In midlife's gentle embrace,
a love affair begins,
a journey of self-discovery,
where self-compassion wins.
With each passing year,
we embrace our flaws,
accepting ourselves fully,
shedding societal applause.
We bloom with love's
tender touch,
appreciating ourselves
so much.

Midlife Happiness

Midlife's happiness,
a radiant light.

We cherish the moments,
both big and small,
In midlife's embrace,
happiness stands tall.
Through laughter and love,
we bask in delight,
Midlife's joy,
an everlasting flight.

Midlife's Symphony

Midlife, a symphony of delight,
Where happiness resides, shining so bright.

Years of wisdom gathered a tapestry we weave,
Contentment is found in moments we believe.

Embracing life's blessings, both big and small,
Midlife's women, finding joy in it all.
With gratitude as our compass, we navigate the days,
Happiness blooms, casting vibrant rays.

In cherished connections and passions pursued,
Midlife's happiness, a treasure renewed.

We dance with laughter, our spirits in flight,
Midlife's embrace, a picture painted in delight.

Midlife Women Together

Midlife women together
a force to be reckoned
In solidarity we stand
our spirits awakened.

With shared experiences
and journeys unique
We find strength together
our bonds ever-sheik.

Embracing our power
shining side by side
Midlife women unite
with courage as our guide.

Midlife Women Unite

Midlife women unite,
a powerful force,
Together we stand,
on a common course.
Through shared experiences,
stories untold,
We create a sisterhood,
resilient and bold.
Bound by strength,
and wisdom we possess,
Midlife women unite,
forever we progress.

A Sacred Bond

Midlife women
A sisterhood formed in a sacred space
Shared experiences
Stories to share
We lift each other
Showing we care

United in resilience, wisdom, and might
Empowering each other,
shining our light.

Sisterhood

In sisterhood, we find our voice,
Supporting each other, making a choice.
To celebrate our journeys, past and present,
Midlife women unite, a force effervescent.

Through challenges faced, we stand tall,
Empowering each other, one and all.

In unity, we conquer, we inspire,
Midlife women unite with hearts afire.

Hooray for Midlife

Hooray for midlife
a season so divine
where confidence
and wisdom intertwine.
Embracing our power
we shine and thrive
Hooray for midlife
it's our time to come alive!

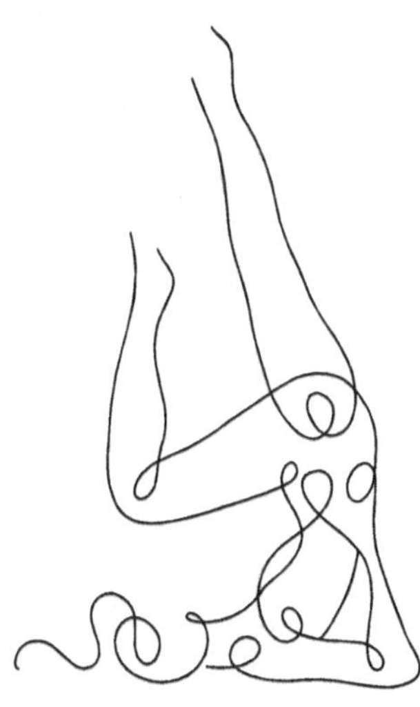

Midlife So Grand

Midlife
a chapter so grand
Where wisdom and beauty,
gracefully stand.
With hearts full of joy
and spirits held high
Midlife's journey
a celebration—oh my!

Shiny Midlife

Midlife, a time to embrace
A time of wisdom,
confidence, and grace.
With hearts aflame,
seize each day.
In midlife,
shine in every way.

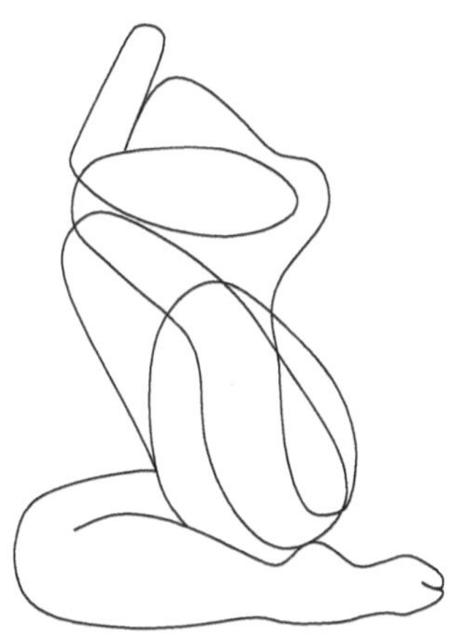

A Cheer for Midlife

Midlife,
a time to cheer
When wisdom grows,
and doubts disappear.
Confidently we stand,
our spirits ablaze,
Embracing the beauty,
of our midlife days.
Strength within,
midlife's journey
A victory
we'll always win.

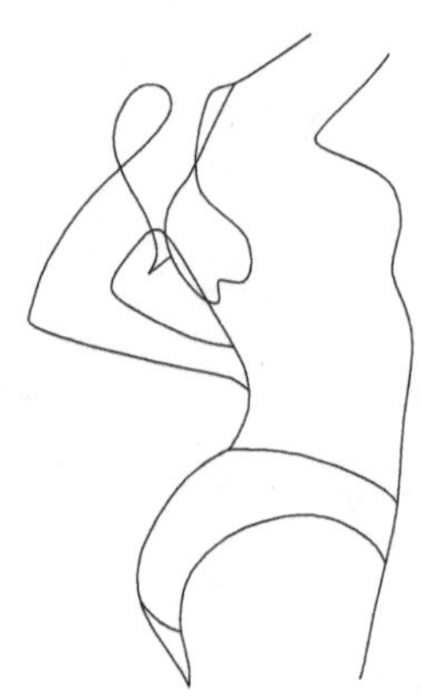

A Shout Out to Midlife

A shout out to midlife
A time to embrace
Where wisdom and beauty intertwine
A glorious case
With hearts full of joy
And spirits aflame
Midlife women,
We celebrate without shame
In this stage of life
We truly thrive
Hooray for midlife,
Where our spirits revive.

The Midlife Race

Through the race of midlife,
we find our joy.
Let us, our passion enjoy.
The path may twist
and challenges arise,
yet we push forward
with unwavering eyes.
Resilience as fuel,
we surpass every pace,
always embracing
our life's grace.

The Winning Stride

We find our winning stride,
Where dreams and aspirations no
longer hide.
With determination and resilience as
our guide,
We conquer obstacles with unwavering
pride.
In the game of life, we claim victory as
our own,
Midlife's champions, empowered and
grown.

Midlife's Light

In midlife's light,
feeling good as can be,
A newfound sense of self,
so wild and free.
With each passing day,
a deeper appreciation grows,
For the beauty of life,
the highs and the lows.
Midlife women,
confident with grace,
Feeling good,
embracing this unique place.

Thriving in Midlife

Midlife, a season where feeling good thrives,
A time when self-discovery truly arrives.

With a newfound wisdom,
and lessons learned,
Feeling good becomes a flame,
that's brightly burned.

Embracing our bodies, minds, and souls,
Midlife's journey,
where feeling good takes control.

Midlife Freedom

In midlife I feel free,
A blossoming season,
finding the true me.

Confidence radiates
from deep within,

Embracing my journey,
letting my true spirit win.

Every moment I cherish
as life's beauty unfurls,

Feeling good in midlife,
embracing the world.

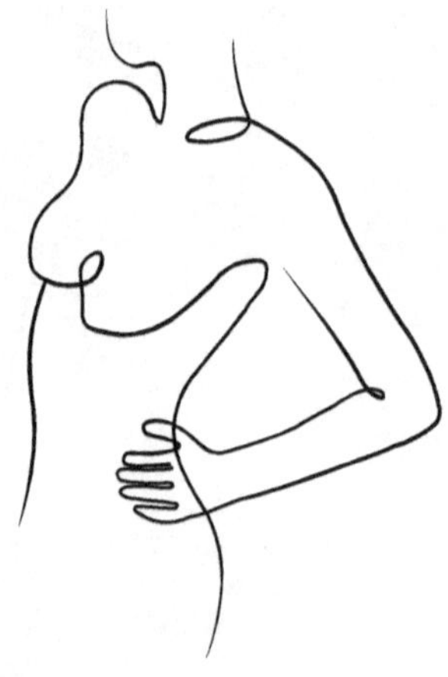

Menopause a Grand Design

Menopause—life's grand design
Where womanhood evolves
like a sacred shrine.
Embracing the flow of the hormonal tide
a chapter where strength and grace collide.
With hot flashes and night sweats
we navigate the change.
Menopause is life
a metamorphosis so strange.
We celebrate the wisdom it bestows
Menopause
a journey where a new self grows.

The Rhythm of Menopause

Life's natural rhythm
a vibrant composition
within a natural transition.
With ebbing tides of hormones
a new path unfolds
embracing the journey
as life gracefully molds.

Menopause Self-Recognition

Menopause, a transformative phase,
in which life's rhythm takes a new embrace.

A natural shift, a profound transition,
Menopause, an invitation to self-recognition.

Embracing the ebb and flow, we find our way,
Menopause,
a testament to resilience each day.

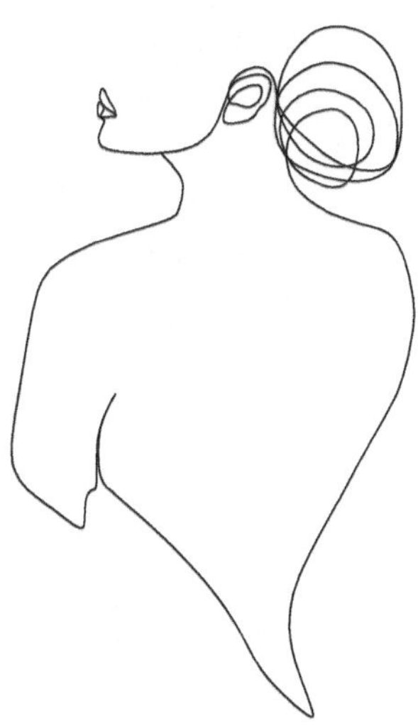

Menopause A Time of Change

Menopause is a time of change and growth
A natural phase where life takes a different oath.

Fluctuating hormones, a tempest of transition
Yet within this storm emerges inner intuition.

Menopause, a journey to embrace
Navigating waves of transformation with grace.

A time to honor the wisdom we hold
Menopause's story,
a tale yet to be fully told.

Menopause's Transformative Tide

Menopause's flowing tide,
We emerge stronger, radiant, with newfound pride.
Embracing the changes,
we stand tall and true,
Better than ever,
in all that we pursue.

With resilience we face each day,
Menopause's journey,
guiding our way.
Celebrating power within our core,
thriving in our essence,
forevermore.

The Arrival of Menopause

Menopause's arrival,
a unique phase,
Where strength and resilience are set ablaze.

Embracing the change,
we rise above,
Better than ever,
fueled by self-love.

With wisdom gained,
and battles won,
Menopause empowers,
a new chapter has begun.

We bloom like never before,
confident and wise—
Menopause's gift,
a radiant rise.

Transforming

Within menopause's changing season,
A woman emerges stronger for a reason.

Though her body changes, a power awakens,
With resilience and grace, she conquers her space.

Better than ever, she rises with pride,
Navigating her midlife journey
Spirit amplified.

Menopause Has Come

Menopause has come

A gateway to transforming.
A time when women rise
reborn and reforming.
Through surging tides
they navigate the waves;
Embracing change
blossoming fierce and brave.

Like rockets, they soar above the flames,
Better than ever, transcending the games.
With newfound wisdom,
and strength in their core,
Menopause's embrace,
a victory they score.

Metamorphosis

Along with menopause
a metamorphosis unfolds
Emerges a strength, a resilience so bold
Though tides may shift
and the body changes it's course
Midlife women rise
embracing their force.

Wisdom's grace and self-discovery's art
midlife women navigate the journey
as a new start.
No longer defined by societal norms
—or expectations—
they find liberation.
Better than ever
they bloom like a flower
unleashing power, hour after hour.

Menopause,
a gateway to newfound bliss
Midlife women
embracing life's passionate kiss.

In the Midst of Menopause

In menopause, a transformation takes place.
Women emerge stronger while spirits embrace.

With wisdom and resilience, they face each trial.
Better than ever, their inner flames ignite.

They redefine beauty beyond youth's fleeting gaze,
Embracing self-love in remarkable ways.

In the midst of menopause, they discover power,
Unleashing their potential, hour by hour.

No longer defined by society's view,
They blossom and thrive, their dreams anew.

Better than ever, they flourish and grow,
Menopause is certainly a time to glow.

Midlife Wisdom

In midlife, wisdom takes hold
A treasure trove of insight
shining so bold.

Through the ebb and flow of hormonal tides
Wisdom blossoms,
as life's tapestry guides.

The Realm of Menopause

In the realm of menopause
wisdom takes flight
like a beacon of light
that guides us through the night.

Through hot flashes and mood swings
a transformation so new

Wisdom blossoms in midlife
as our spirits renew.

Menopause's Embrace

In the depths of menopause's
embrace,
Wisdom whispers with a
gentle grace.

Through the fire of change and
transformation,
A reservoir of wisdom forms, a
cherished revelation.

A Midlife Glow

Midlife
A season of feeling good
Embracing our prime
Radiating confidence
And a spirit sublime.
With self-care our anthem
We nourish body and soul
Embracing wellness
Making ourselves whole
In this chapter of life
We find our inner glow
Feeling good in midlife
A joy we should know

Time Is Strength

Time has woven stories into your eyes
Wisdom's embrace, a treasure undisguised

Graceful lines etched upon your face
Each one is a testament to resilience and grace

Midlife women,
together, we are pillars of strength and might
Radiating beauty and shining bright.

Wise Midlife Women

Wise souls adorned with grace's attire
Each wrinkle tells a tale, a life entire

Time's touch brings beauty, refined and deep
In wisdom's embrace, our spirits leap

Through life's ebbs and flows, we stand tall
Midlife women, let's stay radiant through it all

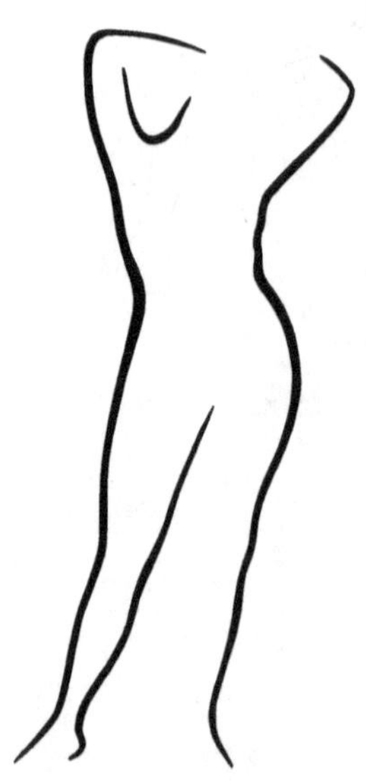

The Golden Years

In the golden years, wisdom does unfold
Stories etched in lines, cherished and bold

With grace and elegance, we stand tall
We are radiant souls who've seen it all

Ageless beauty, a light that transcends
Midlife women are the world's truest friends.

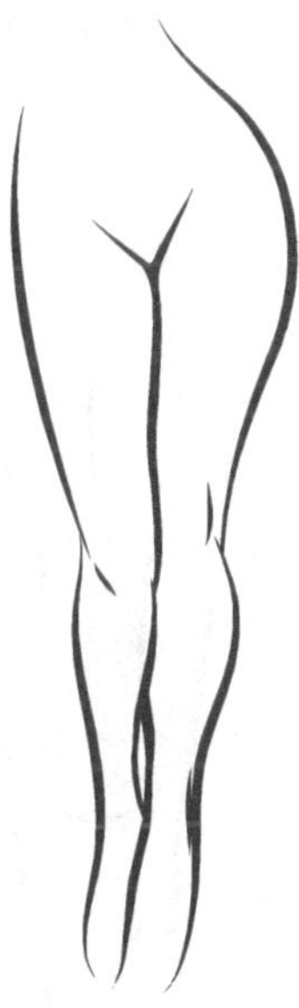

Depths of Time

Within the depths of time,
Midlife women with stories entwined.

A tapestry of strength and grace,
through the lines etched on their weary face.

Through life's journey, they have grown.
Their presence shines, a presence known.

Midlife women are treasures of the soul
Unveiling beauty, making them whole.

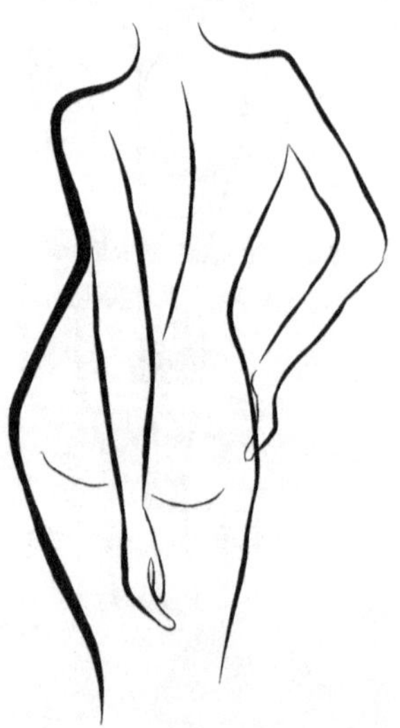

Graceful Aging

Aging gracefully, like rivers deep and wise,
midlife women bloom with beauty in their eyes.

Time's gentle touch paints stories on their face,
each line and wrinkle is a tale of strength and grace.

Experience wields wisdom, tried and true,
with hearts that nurture and souls that still pursue.

Midlife women shine like stars in twilight's gleam,
an inspiration, timeless and serene.

The Midlife Crown

With pride, wisdom's crown they wear
A tapestry of stories beyond compare

Lines of laughter etched upon their face
Each wrinkle holds a tale, a cherished trace

Their souls, resilient, like the ancient trees
Midlife women bloom with life's mysteries

With grace and poise, they shine ever bright
Guiding us through shadows with their love's pure light.

Aging

During age's embrace, wisdom takes hold
Graceful stories of life unfold

Lines etched upon faces, eternally wise
Eyes filled with strength, a spark that defies

With every step, a legacy we create
midlife women, pillars of love and fate.

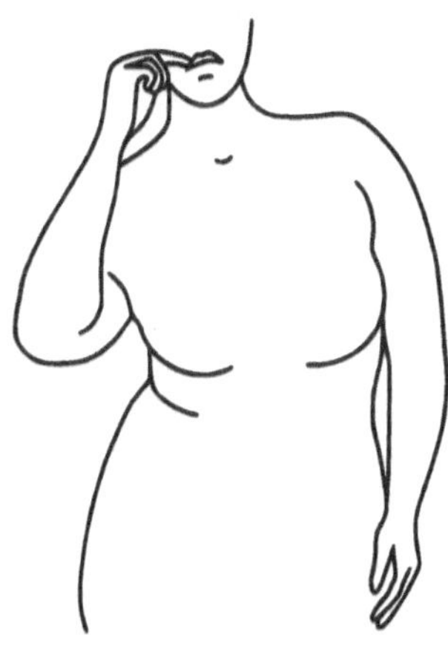

The Twilight's Glow

Within the twilight's glow, there is a woman of grace,
with time's gentle touch resting on her face.

Her eyes have witnessed life's grand tale,
her spirit so strong, it will never pale.

Wisdom etched in each line and crease,
her presence is a symphony of inner peace.

A midlife woman is a beacon of light
that guides us through life's darkest night.

Tapestry of Time

Within the tapestry of time, they shine bright
Midlife women, beacons of wisdom and light

With grace and elegance, they gracefully age
Each line on their face is a life's precious page

Their laughter echoes with stories untold
In their presence, hearts find solace and unfold

Through trials and triumphs, they've come so far
Their strength is bright, like a shining star

With love in their hearts and fire in their souls
midlife women make the wide world whole

Their spirit endures, an eternal flame
A testament to the beauty of age's claim

Midlife Is Like Fine Wine

Aged gracefully, like fine wine,
Midlife women are treasures of the mind.
Each line on their face, a story to tell,
Wisdom and experience, within them, dwell.

Through years of laughter, tears, and strife,
They've blossomed into the fullness of life.
With hearts that overflow with love and care,
Midlife women are icons beyond compare.

Their presence commands respect and awe,
Radiating strength with every step they draw.
In their grace and power, we find inspiration,
Midlife women are the epitome of liberation.

5-Minute Journaling

FEELINGS THAT CAME UP FOR ME WHILE READING THESE POEMS . . .

5-Minute Journaling

HOW I WILL INCORPORATE POSITIVE THOUGHTS INTO MY MIDLIFE JOURNEY . . .

5-Minute Journaling Notes

ACKNOWLEDGMENTS

There are always many people to thank,
and I do so with so much gratitude...

My daughter **Daniella** and cherished granddaughter **Lucy,** may the wisdom within these verses serve as timeless life lessons, guiding you through the phases of womanhood with grace and resilience.

My husband **Eli**, sons **Micky**, **Teddy**, **Jonathan**, **Benjamin**, and my **friends** thank you for your encouragement and for always supporting me in all I do. Most of all, thank you for always making me feel like there is nothing I can't do, cheering me on when I am down, and for your lifelong support.

Brenda and **Leigh,** whose journeys through life's challenges inspire others. Their resilience and positive spirit are a testament to their strength and determination for a new chapter in midlife.

ABOUT THE AUTHOR

Dr. Renata Shiloah, DCN, MS, RD, CDN, RYT, CMT, is a distinguished Doctor of Clinical Nutrition and Integrative Health with over two decades of experience, certified in yoga, meditation, and Usui Shiki Ryoho Reiki. She holds a Bachelor's in Family, Nutrition, and Exercise Science from Queens College CUNY and a Master's in Healthcare Policy and Management and Nutrition from Stony Brook University Medical Center.

Featured in publications like Teen Vogue, Prevention, and SHAPE, Dr. Renata specializes in well-being for midlife women. Her passion for poetry, ignited at age twelve, resulted in "***Poems From the Heart***" and complements her self-help book, "***It's Time for a Pause***." She's also acclaimed for her children's book series, "***Lucy Blue Eyes***."

Born in the Czech Republic and residing in New York City, she's a dedicated advocate of well-being through yoga, meditation, swimming, bike riding, and quality time with her family. Discover the diverse world of Dr. Renata Shiloah, where healing and creativity harmonize.

Discover more at **www.nutritionist4u.com**

OTHER TITLES BY DR. RENATA

'It's Time For A PAUSE'

In addition to **'Poems From The Heart,'** 'It's Time for a **PAUSE'** offers empowering stories from women like you who triumphed over the challenges of menopause. This self-help book presents safe and scientifically proven integrative healing therapies for relieving menopausal symptoms. Unlike conventional approaches that merely address symptoms, such as prescribing medications for joint pain, this book takes a holistic approach by targeting the root causes. By focusing on the underlying factors behind menopausal discomfort and incorporating a healthy diet and integrative healing practices, you'll discover the keys to menopause relief. This resource includes guidance on diet, yoga, meditation, journaling pages, and other tools to support your midlife journey.

'Lucy Blue Eyes: The Series'

'Me And You Together Forever' is the heartwarming beginning of a series that will delight midlife women and their adored grandkids. Follow Lucy, a real-life little girl with captivating blue eyes, on thrilling adventures with her beloved Grandma, known as "Safta-Tata." Page by page, you'll enter a world celebrating generational bonds and the happiness of shared experiences. Prepare to laugh, explore, and create cherished memories with Lucy and Safta-Tata as they remind us that the best adventures are shared with a loved one. This book invites you to rediscover the magic of intergenerational connections and the joy of staying young at heart.

Keep an eye out for these & additional books by Dr. Renata on Amazon and wherever books are sold.